Real
Hay-on-Wye

Other Titles in the Real Series

Real
Hay-on-Wye

Kate Noakes

SERIES EDITOR: PETER FINCH

Seren is the book imprint of
Poetry Wales Press Ltd.
Suite 6, 4 Derwen Road, Bridgend,
Wales, CF31 1LH

www.serenbooks.com
facebook.com/SerenBooks
Twitter: @SerenBooks

ISBN 978-1-78172-577-1

A CIP record for this title is available from
the British Library

The publisher works with the financial assistance
of the Welsh Books Council

Printed in Great Britain by Bell and Bain Ltd, Glasgow

CONTENTS

SOUTH

WEST

SERIES EDITOR'S INTRODUCTION

Castle Street in the fading light. I'm outside the Blue Boar, one of Hay's older hostelries. It is billed tonight as a supper club although it's actually much more like a pub. According to Kilvert's Diaries the stables here housed camels and bears when Wombwell's Menagerie visited in 1872. Tonight though, it's lovers of verse. Hay-on-Wye Booktown is in full flourish. Along with Ifor Thomas and Tôpher Mills I am part of the poetry trio Horses Mouth. Inside the tavern we've been delivering our inimitable performance poetry to a full house of boozy punters who've paid top dollar for a meal ticket to get in. We'd got to that bit in my poem about giving up smoking where my fellow performer Tôpher Mills lights 10 fags simultaneously and the fire alarm has gone off. Irate diners, pint glasses in hand, mill around us in the street, their rapidly cooling Dover sole uneaten inside. The show is done for. The prospect of payment rapidly retreats.

Failed literary events are a Hay exception. Not only is this place the site for Britain's foremost annual literary festival (replete with seasonal outrider events along with half a dozen Hay-bannered replicas abroad) but it is also home to some of the best specialist bookshops in the land. Rugby-educated landowner the late Richard Booth opened the first at the Fire Station on Castle Street in 1962. His achievement is celebrated with a now faded blue plaque outside.

Out of season The Hay, as it is known to older locals, has a population of around 1,600. That makes it about as big as Cardiff at the time of the Black Death. If all its residents attended they wouldn't fill the London Palladium for a matinee. Yet this compact market town manages to attract more than 350,000 visitors annually. Even if it wasn't for the bookshops people would have come. The streets are quaint, aged, crowded with buildings that have hung on here for centuries. There's a cheese and a butter market, a sixteenth century timbered cruck hall and a tumble of ancient streets.

In some usage the Welsh name for The Hay is rendered as Y Gelli Gandryll. This roughly translates as the grove of many pieces. Gandryll might be a latter-day addition to the earlier Y Gelli but it does have a certain ring to it. Not that Hay could ever be described as a pretentious place.

In the centre is a castle. Not the battlements and drawbridge sort but more a fortified manor. It nevertheless did its time as a place of chivalry and sword until history calmed down and regular death became less a matter of everyday life. It was reputed to have been built in a single night by the giantess Maud de St Valery at the end of the thirteenth century. This shambling accumulation of extensions, re-wallings and latter-day additions is currently in the ownership of a Heritage Lottery-aided Trust who purchased it from bookshop king Richard Booth in 2011 and are undertaking refurbishment.

The Honesty Bookshop in the courtyard however, still trades. If trading is the right term. This wonderful invention stacks unsold and usually unsellable volumes on open-air shelves where they sit expanding and flaking in the Welsh weather. If you want you take and if you are honest you leave a coin in one of the collection boxes.

To the south of the medieval castle is the cattle market next to the car park on which once stood a Norman motte. The mound remains visible. Cars strew themselves across what would have been the bailey. In addition to two castles miniscule-sized Hay also once managed to have had walls. They ran in a triangle delineated by Belmont Road, the Wye Valley Walk, and Oxford Road. There were three gates. Nothing remains.

Routes into the town are numerous. On foot you can arrive along the Wye Valley Walk or on top of Offa's Dyke which heads straight for the castle and then vanishes until reappearing northwards beyond the town. It would have been a nice psychogeographic idea to walk into Hay along the Wales-England border but for most of its Hay traverse this runs along the middle of the Dulas Brook. There are a few Hay properties actually in England although most are not. The much larger part of Hay is distinctly in Wales. This is despite its Hereford postcode and total lack of Welsh accent in the local speech.

Greater Hay has proved to be attractive to creatives. Beat poet and master of meditation Allen Ginsberg came to Llanthony in 1967 to write *Wales Visitation*. Turner had painted in the same area in 1792. Bruce Chatwin spent time researching his best-seller *On The Black Hill*, set in countryside just to Hay's east. Eric Gill carved for a living at Capel-y-Ffin. Owen Sheers imagined a failed D Day in *Resistance*, set in the nearby Hay hillscape. Most famously of all the Rev Francis Kilvert was the curate at Clyro where he set his eminently readable and now best-selling diaries. His memorial is nearby at Bredwardine.

These days, though, it is arguable just what has made Hay the more attractive. The Town of Books adventure or the Hay Literature Festival? Both have become super-size draws, marked large on the international calendar.

The Booktown concept has caught alight across the world. Drowning a small place with (mostly) second-hand and antiquarian books might not at first appear to be the best of business plans. Who would buy? Local-economy-enhancing visitors, that's who. Richard Booth's early foray into mass volume retail rapidly took off. To his expanding empire he added shops at the Castle, the Cinema and then at a massive former agricultural merchants. He bought mouldering stately home libraries and publishers' overstocks by the lorry-load. He imported titles by the container-full from right across the English-speaking world. Following the axiom that the best place to open a new shoe shop is next to an existing shoe shop dozens of others set up alongside him.

It helped that Richard Booth was both an eccentric and a great publicist. His proclaiming himself King of Hay and his annexing of the territory and declaring it as independent of the UK in 1977 certainly helped. As did his other antics including the issuing of his own stamps and passports, the nominating of his horse as Hay's first Prime Minister and the creation of transsexual April Ashley as his consort, Hay's first Duchess.

In the hard winter of 1982 he operated a great publicity-generating social service when he offered for free stacks of otherwise unsaleable stock to pensioners. They could use them for warmth by burning them on their stoves. Erotica burned the best, theology the slowest.

Today there are more than twenty bookshops in this place alone. Some have great specialisms. Britain's best (and by now possible only) poetry bookshop is here. Interested in railways? In murder? In antique maps? At Hay you'll be in your element. Hay is twinned with Redu in Belgium, another Booktown, as well as Timbuktu, the great Muslim repository for Arab historical texts. Other Booktowns have been started at nearby Blaenavon and at Wigtown in Scotland as well as in further towns right across the globe.

The Hay's other claim to international fame, the Literature Festival, was created by actor Norman Florence, his wife Rhoda Lewis and their son Peter in 1987. It began in the school and the car park and soon expanded to a field west of town where, today, it has become what Bill Clinton called the 'Woodstock of the mind'. It attracts thousands to a long week of literary and cultural performances and discussions each May.

Over the years the festival has developed a global brand running outlier events in more than thirty locations. From Cartagena in Columbia to cities in Peru, Mexico, Spain and the USA the Hay Festival has brought literature to millions but the big show is still here, at Hay. It is *the* place at which authors appear. If you are in the business you come for the spotlight the Festival affords.

Tony Benn when he was here doing his thermos-flasked tea and avuncular performance of socialist repartee suggested that in his mind Hay 'had replaced Christmas'. Arthur Miller thought Hay-on-Wye to be 'some kind of sandwich'. It's hard to think of many in the literary world's great, good and wannabees who have not attended. The Festival's pushing of the boundaries of what exactly constitutes literature has done them proud. When I came to the first Festival I was a daytime bookseller flogging books out of a car boot at the edge of the car park. At night I'd been given a poetry slot. Not knowing anything about green rooms or, when I now come to think about it, pub toilets, I opted to change standing behind a great pantechnicon on the slowly sloping tarmac. True to expectation the lorry moved while I was in mid trouser change revealing me to a car park full of happy shoppers. I can't say my audience increased in size as a result although I did sell a few more books.

There is something about an economy based on the printed word that marks it as totally different from one based on, say, white goods retail or car part manufacture. The clientele have softer hands. The product they seek generates mental stimulation rather than anything actually physical. Hay feels a safe place, an attractive place, somewhere you want to spend time in. And if the Hay Literature Festival isn't on when you visit, nor the *How The Light Gets In Festival* of Philosophy then look out for the other things this tiny town stages. Food festivals, artisan drink revelries, music gatherings, arts and craft celebrations, horse and pony shows.

Kate Noakes' Hay-on-Wye investigation goes deep into many of these events. She's a poet with all the inventiveness of touch that brings. In true Real style she avoids truck with guidebooks and opts instead for an invigoratingly conversational ramble through the town and its environs. Expect much entertainment and a lot of new knowledge. Real Hay-On-Wye this certainly is.

Peter Finch

PREFACE

I'd been in Paris and France for too long; six years was plenty. It was time for my own personal Brexit. As I was pondering the onerous practicalities of upping sticks, selling my rather swankily located Marais flat, and finding a new job in the UK, I was overtaken by hiraeth, the untranslatable sense of longing for home. More than homesickness, it's something about the smell of damp grass after a shower of fine Welsh rain, the kind that soaks you in minutes, the shiver of wind from the hills and the rough sun on my face, being woken by sheep or a noisy bell. So when the opportunity presented itself to write about home, pick a place, do the work, it seemed too good a chance to miss. I embraced it with willing and grateful arms.

Hay-on-Wye has been one of my spiritual homes since I was a child. Wherever we had been on our holidays: mountain or seashore, or just a family visit, my mother somehow always contrived to have my father point the car the long way round, in the direction of Hay. In the '70s it was the antique shops that I found myself being traipsed around in search of some unrecognised and therefore under-priced treasure. I was pretty bored, but every so often with the excuse of wanting an ice cream

from Shepherd's, I managed to wander off and lose myself in the bookshops to browse, read, and covert gilt-edged bindings.

By then the filthy, nasty books, that Mum was sure harboured disease of some unspecifiable but life-threatening kind, were all over town, as Sommerville[1] has it: "millions and millions of volumes...spilt out and along the streets into converted warehouses, inns, a cinema and other unlikely places, as well as good number of plain ordinary shops." And since I was, and remain a voracious reader, especially after two months' bed rest with asthma when I was twelve, the town looked and felt like my very idea of heaven. It still does. It has been an absolute joy to hang out in Hay, the town of books and festivals and so much more, with the best of all possible excuses. Don't look here if you want a guide to the eateries, pubs and accommodations of Hay. It's not that sort of book. There are plenty of other places where such recommendations can be found. Forgive me then for adding my lovingly intended opinions to the pile of unruly words about Hay and for risking your annoyance, as Francis Kilvert said: "If there is one thing more hateful than another it is being told what to admire and having things pointed out to one with a stick"[2]. I couldn't help myself.

London 2017-19

Like so many things, this poor volume was interrupted by the corona virus pandemic. Between my finishing its final draft and its intended publication date in the spring of 2020, we were locked down. Publication schedules went out of the window, along with festivals and everything else. It has waited patiently until now. I have resisted the temptation to update every single thing, so it may, in places, be already historic, but it is an affectionate record of my favourite town in Wales nonetheless and I don't think this should spoil your enjoyment.

London 2022

"What's Hay-on-Wye? Some kind of sandwich?"
– Arthur Miller

INTRODUCTION

There's an old Hay saying that goes something like: if you stand on the walls of Hay castle and throw an iron bar east into England and come back to find it after a year, it will have grown into an apple tree. If you throw the bar west, you will hit a sheep. Hereford's apple orchards are testament to that, perhaps, and yes, there are sheep aplenty in Wales.

I am walking into town having just been shopping in the Co-op on Newport Street on the easterly fringe of Hay. I've just left England. The border is that close in so many places near town. Most English people I know think Hay is in England – I had to correct someone on Facebook just the other day. England, the place where my great-grandmother only once ventured during her whole, relatively long life. In the early 1960s, she counselled my soon-to-be-emigrating parents to be careful with the English. Anyone would have thought they were going to the other side of the world. We did that later, but that's another story

Much is made of the old rivalry between the Welsh and the English, by the Welsh who in varying degrees hate or dislike the English, and by the English, who when they think of us at all consider us variously stupid, sheep-obsessed and worse, dishonest, or frankly beneath notice. It preys on my mind sometimes that I seem to have failed as a parent: my daughters are half English and they don't consider themselves to be even the slightest bit Welsh, despite their names. My sister seems to have done a better job with her half-English sons. Given the chance, one would play rugby in a red jersey. This half-pleases my father.

Mostly such banter is good-natured these days, except the unsurprisingly outraged reaction when an English Archbishop recently suggested the Welsh sing God Save the Queen at sporting fixtures, or perhaps on the one Saturday in February or March each year when fifteen of theirs in white shirts and fifteen of ours in red run out onto a field and battle it out with the right-shaped ball. It is said that when you play the Welsh, you are not playing a rugby team, but a nation. True. It's that important. When I was married to an Englishman, we had to watch the match on different televisions in different parts of the house, and one or other of us was bound to be in a foul mood for the rest of the weekend. Others go to great efforts to be in the right place for the game. My childhood dentist used to drive over the Severn bridge from Bristol to his parents' home in Cardiff as he would not be able to enjoy it otherwise. I know what he meant. I had much joy watching the Wales victory over England in the last World Cup from a sofa in Cardiff. I swear I could hear the whole city cheering. And our unbroken run of international wins in recent years is a source of much pride. As I write, we don't seem to know how to lose (well, not often).

Flat holm / Steep holm

Too Welsh for the English
Too English for the Welsh,
sometimes it seems I should make my home
in the middle of the Severn estuary
with oozings and miles of mud,
to be drowned twice a day in the brisk tide
as punishment or reminder that I am
Too English for the Welsh
Too Welsh for the English.

But I am all oyster catcher
and sand eel, stunted grass and drift,
flat-topped and steep-sided on my

island-home sanctuaries come prisons,
places reserved for those who are
Too Welsh for the English
Too English for the Welsh,
where all kinds of gull call and cry,
but cannot teach me the anthem's words.

I am wild peony and golden samphire,
Buck's plantain and wild leeks
snaked about by slow worms, blue
in their markings like the sea.
I am crane's bill and trefoil, stone crop
and rock lavender, all the colours
of land and sky, yet still
Too English for the Welsh
Too Welsh for the English.

I say mostly, but a language controversy did rear its head in Hay in 2019. A tweet from a Welsh-speaking visitor to the Oxfam shop reported that he and his family were allegedly told by one of the shop staff to get out of the shop and stop speaking that bloody foreign language. With no first-hand knowledge, I make no comment on the veracity of this, but it was denied and later found to be unsubstantiated. The result over a two year period though was a public apology from Oxfam Cymru, the shop being closed and its locks changed, and a complete change of staff in the shop by 2021, including long-standing volunteers who either left in

protest at Oxfam's handling of the situation and other changes to the charity's operational plans, or were un-volunteered. The story even made the national press.[3] It is a sad tale all round and for all involved.

Long gone, thankfully, are the systematic attempts to eradicate the Welsh language as means of encouraging the preferable learning of English. My grandparents were the last to suffer the ignominies of the Welsh Not. If you are beaten in school for speaking Welsh, you soon stop. This is why they passed on very little of it to my parents, and thus hardly any of its words are at home on my tongue. On her deathbed my great-grandmother forgot, wilfully or otherwise, how to speak English, which made life rather tricky for her carers. My last memory of her is of us trying to communicate; she thought I was my mother. I tried and failed to tell her I was not.

Yet, actual fighting not withstanding, England and the English have seemed to dominate Hay for many years, even in something as infuriatingly simple as the postcode. Royal Mail in its wisdom has given Hay a series of Hereford postcodes. This means that, not only does it think Hay is in England, so does everyone else relying on the information; Google, for example, along with more than one visitor to the Hay Festival. The truth, as any decent map will have drawn it, is that Hay is in Powys (Brecknockshire in old money[4]), and in Wales. Good luck trying to convince the interweb of that apparently minor detail.

But perhaps English domination today is too strong a description given Hay's size and relative insignificance. According to Peter Conradi[5], Hay is "ignored or forgotten by the English as too remote, and by the Welsh as too English". A survey made in 2001[6] found, with great precision, that 88.66% of the inhabitants of Hay had no knowledge of Welsh at all. This makes Hay the most linguistically anglicised community in Breconshire. I am always surprised to hear so very few Welsh accents, let alone Welsh words, on the streets of Hay and in its shops. Walking down Castle Street I hear plenty of English voices, everywhere, and even Irish and American ones. A market pastry chef hails from Northern Ireland, and the owner of Booth's bookshop is American. One of her countrywomen brought me my cappuccino last time I was there. So, I have to put away my few polite phrases of Welsh and save them for another place further from the border.

Fairly predictably in my endeavours to write this book I have been rereading the diary of Francis Kilvert, the curate of Clyro, the small village one mile to the north of Hay, and probably the area's most famous literary adoptive son. From time to time he pops up with observations that are still prescient. I enjoy his unpretentious observations and the rather coy way he talks about young ladies. He makes several references to English and Welsh culture rubbing up against one another at various places in his diary. First on Friday 18 November 1870 reporting a conversation about parish boundaries he tells "the extraordinary story…about the birth of a child in this house (the Pant) and the care taken that the child should be born in England in the English corner of the cottage. 'Stand here in the corner,' said the midwife. And the girl was delivered of the child standing."

Kilvert makes no further comment, nor, tantalizingly does he explain why the mother was so keen that her child be born in England. Perhaps the perceived advantages of an English birth were so obvious at the time of his writing that he did not need to spell them out to himself; his diaries were after all not written for publication. I can only shrug, smile wryly, and think of the poor mother giving birth in what sounds like a considerable degree of discomfort.

In jest, but yet still noteworthy, Kilvert writes on 13 November 1871 of an overhearing: "What a fine day it is. Let us go out and kill something". The old reproach against the English. "The Squire has just gone by with a shooting party".

Bruce Chatwin takes up the idea and significance of the border running through houses in his 1982 novel *On the Black Hill*. He has it run down the middle of the staircase in the farm called The Vision where his protagonists live. Later he emphasises the importance of country and border, as the twin brothers, Lewis and Benjamin Jones, are taken by their grandfather on either the English walk, or the Welsh walk.

Mischief can be made, and why should I not, from the confusions of language in terms of even the town's name. The Welsh Encyclopaedia explains that the Hay derives from the old English, *(g)haeg*, originally meaning a fence, then later meaning part of a hunting forest enclosed by fences. Other sources, including the Hay Preservation Trust's plaque, give it as deriving from the Norman French, *haie*, meaning a walled or fenced enclosure. So far so, sort of, consistent you might think. The Welsh name, *Y Gelli*, however means the grove in English. Nothing then to do with fences *per se*, and so the precision we crave these days in knowing things for definite is allusive. In any case, none of these words is in any way related to the dry grass fed to animals.

Kilvert provides an amusing anecdote of things being lost in translation[7] and heads hung in church as a result. One of this temporary assistant curates apparently had such shaky Welsh that in publishing the banns for a hapless couple he asked: "Why these two backsides may not be lawfully joined in Holy Matrimony". But joking aside, let's just be clear that I never ask for a full English breakfast in Hay, even if that is how it is advertised at Oscar's Bistro. Not ever. No, when choosing from the comprehensive and correctly named selection in The Granary by the Clock Tower, or when asking for off menu variants, I have Welsh eggs with my avocado on gluten free toast. *Diolch yn fawr* (Thank you very much).

On May day 1872 Kilvert came home about midnight over Rhydspence border brook and noted the difference between the English celebrations and the more sober Welsh, as the "English Inn was still ablaze with light and noisy with songs and revellers, but the Welsh Inn was dark and still". These days I can't believe that any such distinction could be drawn and indeed Kilvert doesn't fail to mention the rowdiness of Hay and Clyro's taverns on plenty of other occasions. Drink and young men with things to argue about are also the recipe for the fighting at more than one of the Young Farmer's events Oliver Balch[8] reports on in his chapter of the same name. I can't say I've witnessed any such unruliness, other than the raucous singing of *Delilah* by the patrons of the Rose and Crown spilled outside onto the street on a Saturday night. But perhaps *plus ça change*, until it does, as the Rose and Crown is now closed.

Shabby land-song[9]

So sigh here, or shine then my straight stretch of sea,
all slate and silver shod, my shrapnel rocks stacked
slant, my shy grass shivery before the scythe,

my schist and sliver of sky, its shawl of cloud,
my shut sorrel path and strew-stone slopes,
my roadside shrine of squid graffiti, shade signs
of stag and toad, my sheep shank swimming,

shingle squeaks and shale sand shouts, the shift
and shunt of skin shoulders in me among a thousand
shuddering voices, show singing or swan shrieking
from small sheets of hearth, heath, health.

EAST

NEWPORT STREET – HOUSES, NOT EXACTLY AFFORDABLE

The trouble with being a nice place – historic, visually appealing, quiet and surrounded by spectacular scenery kind of nice – with a lot going for it, is that people from all over the country want to come and live in Hay. Incomers hail from more affluent everywhere, even other countries. This pushes up house prices, which in and around the town are significantly higher than the villages a fifteen minute car journey away. All very well if you can afford the 'Hollywood' of Cusop Dingle, but when a small studio apartment in town costs, give or take, a hundred grand, local young people simply cannot set up home here. There's the twin problem: insufficient jobs opportunities outside of retail, light engineering, healthcare, and, of course, agriculture, none of which are famed for their fabulous salaries; and an insufficient supply of housing. You might think that with all the houses that have been built in Hay in the last twenty years, both infilling parts of the town and extending its boundaries, the latter problem was being dealt with, but it's not. This is not a unique Hay problem, of course, repeated as it is across the ever-greying countryside, but here it is writ somewhat large.

So it is with a little hope in my heart that I look at Acorn Property's newly broken ground on Newport Street. The rich red soil covering the site is being moulded into heaps, foundations dug and a development of twenty-five houses, rather tackily and unimaginatively named Bookers Edge, is beginning to rise in brick and wooden cladding. But hardly any of these homes fall into the affordable for local people category, even if they have been designed to reflect Victorian style, unlike the six new houses recently built in Clyro, all of which do.

HERE COMES THE CHOPPER TO CHOP OFF YOUR HEAD

A few yards on from the Co-op and a puzzle presents itself. The large brick buildings on the opposite side of Newport Street, and now a weigh station and Hay and Brecon Farmers supply store, are, what exactly? Well, an engine shed, and one the remnants of the railway that came to Hay in 1864. The two notable other such buildings are the Station Stores, which is one property in a row of Victorian red and yellow brick, now a private house and prior to being a shop, was the stationmaster's house; and the river walk that runs along the southern bank of the Wye where the railway track was. It's all rather past tense. A pity, as rural areas, and Hay is no exception, are much in need of reliable, plentiful and environmentally friendly public transport.

For over a hundred years Hay had the benefit of rail transport in two forms. As early as 1811 Parliament approved the building of a horse drawn trackway – steam locomotives were a gleam in Stephenson's eye until the late 1820s – between the Brecon canal some ten miles to the east of Hay, via Hay, to Eardisley some dozen or so miles to its north east. It took five years until 1816 to build the forty-two inch gauge rails on stone planks to Hay. The trackway then opened in stages on to Clifford Castle in 1817, and Eardisley in 1818. In 1820 it was extended to join the Kington tramway, adding a further twelve miles to the existing twenty-four and making the longest trackway in the UK at the time. Intended to carry goods and freight, with passengers, unofficially, if at all, it was a vital link for trade along this stretch of the Wye valley. By 1860 the tramway was absorbed into the Hereford, Hay and Brecon Railway, which used part of its route, and it was converted to standard gauge (fifty-six and a half inches) for use by steam trains, opening in 1864. By this time the network of steam railways across the UK was extensive. Hay, being remotely located, was somewhat late to the party but, hey, if it ain't broke.

Built by Thomas Savin (1826-1889), a prominent railway engineer from Oswestry in Shropshire, who had constructed many lines in Wales and the Marches, the Hereford, Hay and Brecon Railway struggled financially, much like its owner. Savin became bankrupt in 1866, not that this minor detail stopped him becoming Mayor of Oswestry that very year. The railway was taken over by the Midland Railway enabling it to put together the Birmingham to Swansea line. Hay also had a junction added when the Golden Valley Railway was built between 1876 and 1889 linking the town to Pontrilas, but this line closed in 1898, again presumably because, well, money.

Dr Richard Beeching's 1963 report *The Reshaping of British Railways* operating on the premise that railways should run at a profit saw the closure of 5000 miles of track and 2,363 stations across the UK. Hay's was one of them. There was protest, including from visitor to Hay[10], the later Poet Laureate, John Betjeman. Known for his celebration of amongst other things, the railways, he was the most prominent member of the Railway Development Association. But Beeching, the most hated civil servant in Britain, entertained no romantic notions of the value of railways to our national identity, let alone any thought that they might have a social imperative, as MP Barbara Castle persuaded Parliament a decade later in ensuring their subsidy. No, it was financial losses, the development of road transport, or as Betjeman had it in a letter to the government "the diesel-scented traffic jams"[11], and the growth in car ownership that did for them.

Astonishingly, there was no coherent plan for the redevelopment of the railway land, some of which was built on, turned back to agriculture, or allowed to become derelict. Hay was lucky, as a beautiful walk opened itself up. It is a cool, shady refuge on a hot day and shelter from the rain on the more frequent wet ones, when water dripping from the leaves almost drowns out the Wye as it babbles over its gravel beds. Unlike Betjeman's longings, such as in the last stanza of 'Dilton Marsh Halt', where he writes[12]:

And when all the horrible roads are finally done for,
And there's no more petrol left in the world to burn,

Here to the Halt from Salisbury and from Bristol
Steam trains will return

I would not want lose this linear park of green, but can't help wondering how much easier life would be at festival time if the tracks were not gone. And how much more eco-friendly a new train to Hereford would be. There is though no reopening plan for Hay, nothing like the new lines linking the towns and valleys to Cardiff further south.

BROAD STREET – WHERE ALL THE WORLD'S A STAGE

Joining Newport Street and taking you into the centre of town, it's hard to tell exactly where Broad Street starts. Perhaps it is at the site of the walled-up town well on the left at the foot of the short calf-aching hill. Perhaps it's opposite the well at the white painted house where a plaque announces the remnants of one of the town gates, or perhaps the junction with Wye End Road marks the spot. Even if not there, this as good a place as any to pause for a moment.

My shopping bags are weighing down my arms. As usual I forgot I didn't bring the car and have bought so much more than I can actually carry. I want to get back, but need to rest, so I seek the sanctuary of a great cup of coffee in one of Hay's key cultural spaces, The Globe[13], also known as the iai, or Institute of Art and Ideas. The Globe was a former Methodist chapel, the Ebenezer United Reform Church, and was converted into an arts centre in 2008 by the philosopher, Hilary Lawson. He originally came to Hay for its peace and quiet as a place to write. He was not the first person to do so and certainly will not be the last. Known for his theory of closure of the human experience, the book of the theory by the same name which was published in 2001 and took him a decade to write while he was busy pursuing a media career.

A true polymath, in the 1980s and 1990s Lawson was an editor and deputy chief executive at TV-am and founder of production company TVF Media and editor of Channel 4's *The World This Week*, and other documentary work. He explains his focus on work in the media because he sees these as the public spaces where ideas are discussed and their impact on the world examined.[14] The

BFI lists over 200 film credits for him, including a *Palm D'Argent* from Cannes. He has had many film and TV prize nominations. Lawson was creator of the first video paintings in 2001 and founder of an artists' collective, Artscape, to explore the medium, also working with programmers on suitable storage software. He considers video painting a practical means of escaping closure and approaching openness, and his work has been shown amongst other places at The Hayward Gallery and ICA in London, and, of course, The Globe. This is the kind of impressive CV that is hard to credit to one person. Any one of these would be considered an achievement for us mere mortals. He is quite something.

The Globe is an independent art centre staging art exhibitions, live music, films, talks and debates, courses and workshops and the like. It has even been kind enough to have me run a writing workshop for them. It is a charitable trust dedicated to freethinking, creativity and debate. It tries to be as socially inclusive as possible running events for schools, and talks on environmentalism and Buddhism. This is the place to come if you want to learn Spanish in Hay.

Stirring my cappuccino (£2.50 and the best in Hay imho btw), I am alone in the upstairs main room of the chapel proper. The Gothic pulpit has been repositioned and its paling oak now sits in the corner of the space. The seating is chic Welsh blanket upholstered chairs distressed into shabbiness, and the odd leather armchair, similarly. The banquettes are raspberry velour with satin and blanket cushions, and as with everywhere in town, there is a bookcase full of books for sale, and a good solid table for me to write at. Art films are projected onto one of the huge walls and its opposite is painted deep plum. Today it's a film of night-time London. Naturally, I turn my back to it. I'm in Hay and loving it and not wanting to be reminded of home just now.

There is something to entertain at The Globe every day of the week from music to theatre, to talks and open mic, a Philosophy café, and even a Lego club. And the bar serves a selection of fine ales. You can even come here to work at the monthly Friday Freework session. Imagine that anywhere else – a place to set up your computer for free and network with other freelancers for the price of a few drinks and snacks. It's not a business model that many co-working spaces adopt, that's for sure. Downstairs its restaurant is home to the Off-Grid Gourmet, and there are additional once a month supper club dinners. The food is as locally sourced as possible, for which I have no hesitation in awarding them lashings of brownie points.

Every time I have been here it has been packed with locals and visitors alike and the evenings hugely entertaining, and importantly not straining on the purse. Tuesday (now Friday) is Open Mic night, where the talent of Hay gets to strut its stuff. Hosted by Chris Bradshaw, book binder and editor of the Hay poetry magazine, Quirk, it's a mix of spoken word and music, mainly music, of a wide range and very high quality. Everyone has ten minutes to perform to a forgiving crowd. Bum notes and forgotten words are overlooked. Things are well organised as there is a roving sound engineer on hand to make sure everyone is showcased to their best advantage whether they are singing their own compositions or covering others'. And it's free, but one should never expect it to start on time, or anything like.

Right now though, as my coffee cools, The Globe is quiet enough to hear a creak of wind through the great tree in its garden and to fancy one can hear the ivy growing in through the windows unobserved. Built in 1845, it is a solid stone building with five arched windows and a lovely arched front door. It looks almost Georgian, despite the date of its construction, so semi-classical in that way. Its first minister was one David Griffiths (1792-1863), whose claim to fame was his missionary ministry in Madagascar and his work translating the Bible into Malagasy. Griffiths hailed from Carmarthenshire and in 1820 was sent with another preacher, David Jones, by the London Missionary Society to Madagascar where they set up the first protestant mission. The Society was formed in 1795 to "spread the knowledge of Christ among heathen and other unenlightened nations."[15] Along with preaching and establishing tens of schools on the island, Griffiths and Jones devised a Roman alphabet for the Malagasy language. In 1827 having obtained a printing press, over the next year they supervised the printing of school books, the catechism, a hymnal, and St John's Gospel. By 1831 the whole of the New Testament had been translated and published, along with much of the Old Testament. This is noteworthy as the first publication of the Bible in any African language.

Successful though the mission was from the missionaries' point of view, it did not always meet with approval of the Madagascan royal family and its advisors. In 1828 when King Radama I died, there was a period of uncertainty as to whether the mission would survive. In 1832 Queen Ranavalona, his successor, bowed to pressure from certain of her ministers, and ordered the closure of the mission. It survived by virtue of her change of heart, but in 1835 fierce anti-Christian activity meant Griffiths and Jones decided to leave the island. Ironically though a couple of years' later Griffiths was invited back, but as a merchant, not a missionary. He returned in 1838 only to be charged for aiding the flight of Christian Malagasy citizens. His initial death sentence – seems a bit stiff – was, because he was a foreigner, commuted to a fine. Not surprisingly he scarpered for the last time in 1842. It seems strange to me that, faced with hostility and violence, anyone would want to go back to a potentially dangerous place. I guess missionary zeal is something I don't understand, not in the slightest, but looking at a portrait of Griffiths – a slick of thick black hair, large nose, and stiff collar and tie below his unsmiling face – I note his index finger pointing out a Bible passage. His stare is intense and his visage serious, bordering on the scary; the kind of portentous look that might frighten one into conversion.

Griffiths, the scholarly man, somewhat unsurprisingly added to his writing credits in 1841 with *Persecuted Christians of Madagascar*, which was published in London. He settled with his family in Hay in 1842 waiting the opening of the Congregational church in 1845, probably living in Rock House across the street from it. It seems his pen did not lie idle, as he was busy on his *History of Madagascar.* Between 1850 and 1856 he worked alone on revisions to the Malagasy Bible at the request of the London Missionary Society, along with more works of grammar, catechisms, hymn books, and almost a dozen treatises. Life in Victorian Britain was a tough though and like so many families, Griffiths' had its share of personal tragedy. His son Ebenezer, also a Minister, died of the all-too-common tuberculosis aged 25 in 1852, of which Griffiths wrote in *Copy of a Memorandum*:

> A father's anxious solicitude was extended, a mother's warmest love was lavished – sisters taxed every ingenuity to instigate his pain (??) and all endeavoured by the soft wooings of love to keep back his Spirit, but all in vain.

Which is almost a poem, if one were to lineate it around the 'ed' and 'ain' rhymes, and might have been an epitaph for Ebenezer's grave in the Hay chapel yard. Within the succeeding six years three of the Griffiths adult daughters had also died. Perhaps this loss of family propelled his final move to Machynlleth in 1858 and where he died in 1863. I imagine Hay's congregation a lucky one to have had such a well-travelled and well-educated minister in its new chapel, but what did he think of Hay? I can only guess he might have found it a little unexciting after his adventures in the tropics, or perhaps not, the drive to be comfortable and at home at a certain point in one's life is one with which I can identify.

ILLUMINATION

Part philosophy lecture, part music festival, and tiny part funfair, *How the Light Gets In*, is a sort of rival festival to the rather more famous Hay Festival, although it is doing quite different things. It was founded by Lawson and is described as the European TED, although with one big difference in that it provides debates and not simply a platform for its speakers. The festival site is located at the eastern end of town in a riverside field behind the Co-op, which is a more picturesque setting that it sounds. Curiously it takes place on the same first weekend as the other festival. I would have thought that different timing would allow people to come to the delights of Hay again, at another time of the year. No-one seems very sure about the reasons for the co-incidence. Most locals agree that the timing concentrates the disruption to town life, and the noise and nuisance created by so many visitors into just a couple of weeks, after which, the Hay folk who have worked their socks off catering for us all can lie down in a dark room and take a long and very well-deserved rest.

Now just four days long, *How the Light Gets In* is organised by the iai and presents a bewildering concentration of debates on philosophical and political topics, attracting speakers including eminent academics from all over the world, well known politicians and some of our best journalists. As Lawson has explained, it is an event to talk about the things that matter, a real conversation about big ideas and how to apply and move them on. 2019's festival had me listening to the likes of Terry Eagleton, Philip Blond, Yasmin Alibhai Brown, David Aaronvitch, David Blunkett and Liz Truss, to name but a few. It is a wonderful melange of sometimes brain-aching intellectual content – that'll be me trying to follow a debate on stoicism – animated and anger-making political discussion, with evenings of comedy and toe-tapping music.

As festivals go it is small and perfectly formed, but although the food and drink is a good quality selection, it is not exactly cheap, and the camping, like camping at any festival involves going to sleep in a disco and trying to stay asleep as noisy drunk people stumble about arguing and looking for their tents. That element aside, I came away with a head full of ideas to think and read about for the next several months, and revisit if I want to on the iai's online TV channel. Exhausting and inspiring. And green. Green, green, green, and I don't just mean the excellent recycling and provision of not-plastic cups. Sitting in a stripy deckchair by the river my vision was filled with all shades of green; that gentle softness that delights as much as the Wye's fast flowing waters, troubled enough over small bands of rock to make a passing paddle-boarder kneel on his board and concentrate a little harder, but not so hard as to stop him smiling and waving.

As with everywhere you go in Hay, people talk to one another at the festival; that is rather the point, continuing the debate after its rather short time is over. And as someone once told me in the supermarket, Hay is a gem, everyone talks to everyone, rich or poor; come here for a while if you are feeling low and you'll leave much better. The same can very much be said about *How the Light Gets In* as curious and thinking people from all over the country, and beyond – I spoke to visitors from the Netherlands and the US – beat a path to it. Hay folk are very lucky to have this one, and the offer of half-price tickets. Not that I'm jealous or anything. Although wait, the festival has a London edition in September at Kenwood House in Hampstead, without the discount, of course.

WHAT CASH MACHINE?

On Broad Street's high pavement, hidden by the lime trees, one of the Georgian houses used to be Barclays Bank. I say used to be because it closed in June 2018, the last of the town's three banks to do so. HSBC shut up shop years ago, and its building on Memorial Square has been converted into a rather nice ladies' clothes shop. NatWest followed suit in October 2017, with the dubious honour of last cash withdrawal going to author and Clyro resident, Jasper Fforde. Its building is going to become a recording studio, perhaps one day. Online banking is to blame, but this is of no help to those who can't use computers, or who actually want to withdraw and spend cash. The only options now are the Yorkshire

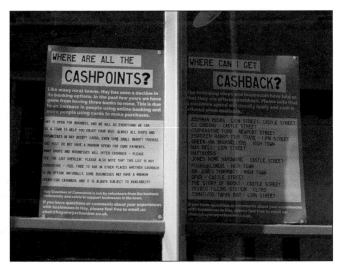

across the road from Barclays, but that's a building society not a bank, or the Co-op, (but that was ram raided at Easter 2019 and the entire cash machine taken), or the Post Office, if you like queuing when its cash machine is not working. And even the Post Office has now gone, as its Postmaster of thirty-five years, Steve Like, wanting to retire, tried to sell it without success and finally hung up his shingle in 2021. Its cash machine remains and a small Post Office service is available in Country Stores, but it's not the same. Often shopkeepers decline cash in these days of contactless payments. It's simply too difficult to bank it.

It is a sad choice that banks make to un-serve isolated communities citing lack of use by locals, whilst simultaneously forgetting their customers who, as tourists or festivalgoers, visit Hay. Banks are not public services, I know that, but just sometimes, dreamer that I am, it would be heartening to think that profit might be forgone for community. Don't banks have corporate responsibility programmes that actually mean just that? I must have missed the memo. Wait, I take it back, sort of. The NatWest mobile van does come to Hay, but just once a week, on a Friday, for a whole forty-five minutes. Wow. Thank goodness for the cash back scheme generously run by so many of Hay's businesses. This means you have to make a purchase though. So, smaller cheer, but a hey, they are not banks, just public-spirited enterprises trying to prop up the town's economy where the big boys have failed it.

Creeping ruralism is the largest problem for Hay noted by local auctioneer, now disgraced, and now former, MP, Chris Davies, who lives four miles away from Hay to its west at Glasbury. From 2015 when he unseated the long sitting Liberal Democrat MP, Roger Williams, Davies had the honour of representing the largest constituency in England and Wales when I spoke to him, before his conviction for making false expense claims. He is only the second MP to be so unseated, ever. Some nineteen per cent of the electorate, over 10,000 people, signed the petition calling for him to lose his seat. This forced by-election in August 2019, in which, incredibly, he was given the Conservative nomination once more and that saw him lose to Liberal Democrat, Jane Dodds. The swing from Conservative to Lib Dem was over 14% and reduced the Conservative government's majority to just one seat. Aided by an alliance of non-standing Greens and Plaid Cymru, Dodds took over 43% of the vote. She served for just a few months and was unseated by Fay Jones in the Tories' sweeping victory in December 2019.

Brecon and Radnorshire is 85 miles long and Davies explained ruralism in terms of bald economics. Lack of transport infrastructure makes the bus service and the dial-a-ride[16] volunteer service a lifeline, especially for the elderly population. Hay is still a place where people look after their own, but there is something about the kind of reliance on the Conservatives' notion of harnessing the third sector that sticks in my throat. Basic things should be available regardless of the size of the population; jobs being another one. Hay has relied on agriculture and tourism as the mainstays of its economy, Richard Booth, the self-proclaimed King of Hay, founder of a secondhand bookshop empire and inventor of the book town, having done an amazing job propping up a dying market town, according to Davies. Yes, there is the pill factory too, but those aside, work is sometimes hard to find for the young, who are forced to move away. And these days, high-speed reliable broadband is essential, but not ubiquitous in Hay.

It's a familiar tale the country over and unlikely to improve any time soon as we witness the disappearance of EU subsidies, to be replaced with who knows what as a result of the catastrophe that is Brexit. You get what you vote for, and that has never been so true in Wales at present. I am astonished that my countrymen and women didn't twig that the blue sign with the circle stars outside the village means cash and continuity of rural life, and as for farming subsidies, do they really think these will continue? I take no pleasure in predicting the demise of hill sheep farming. I wonder what Davies, when he was on it, and his ilk on the Select Committee for Environment, Food and Rural Affairs will want to do about that. Things, including the management and preservation of the countryside, let alone people's livelihoods, are only going to get much worse.

ON A COLD NIGHT, THIS IS THE WARMEST PLACE IN TOWN

The Hay Festival Winter Weekend, the November three day edition of the more well-known May literary festival, is in full swing. Having sat in a barely heated tent all afternoon, I am cold, so cold it has seeped into my very bones. Not quite as cold as the day, aged eleven, when I stubbornly refused to put on proper clothes as I was enthralled by something, I remember not what, on TV and became so cold my lips actually turned blue, but not far off. I am hungry. I need to eat and warm myself back to room temperature. There is nothing so tempting as a steamy, freshly fried pile of chips, ready to be dipped in ketchup. None of your mayonnaise, cheesy chips or curry sauce, thank you. An everyday staple for many people, chips are actually a treat for me. When I have the chance, I rather enjoy smacking my greasy lips. Thus it's to the chip shop I go in search of both sustenance and free heat.

Waiting at Terri's Hay Takeaway on Broad Street I glue my hands to the glass and steel cabinets containing battered fish, pies, sausages and the like. I keep them where they are and only move them very slowly as the early evening customers inch up the queue. By the time I am being served I've decided to stick to the classic small fish and chips. I've considered and eschewed a variety of other things that just somehow are not tempting enough. I don't really like Chinese food.

Pickled eggs, as tradition demands, sit in a huge glass jar on the counter looking like a potential alien life form, and for a moment I have a nightmarish flashback to school cookery lessons and the dreaded instructions on how to prevent black rings forming around our egg yolks. These had something to do with cooling the boiled eggs slowly and not being too quick to run them under the cold tap. Black rings were a mark of failure. Thankfully I am quickly brought back to the now by my parcel of salted and vinegared delight, and with can of fizzy drink – another usual no-no – and enough sachets of tomato sauce to smother every chip, I am half way to my goal. I step through the open door, the only one that can afford to be so in town tonight, and dash through the freezing air to a warm hearth.

ABSOLUTELY EVERYTHING IS FOR SALE

This is how the Old Electric Shop and café on Broad Street explains itself, even the old school lab stool I am sitting on. This destination with its white, white walls, stripped floorboards, and state of the art coffee machine would not look out of place in Shoreditch. In winter globes of mistletoe hang from the roof beams and it twinkles with a thousand lights. In summer the vintage shop within the shop is full of Hawaiian shirts and sunglasses. All year it sells a great mixture of handmade furniture, jewellery, clothes, prints and home wares. Pairs of beeswax candles in all shapes and sizes hang over a red curtain pole. These are not the sorts of things you actually need to buy on a day–to-day basis, but the kind of goods that are nice to look at, temptations to treat, as one of my lawyer friends might say, and priced accordingly. I've often coveted a tweed cushion that comes replete with, what else, but a seemingly useful, though probably vestigial, book pocket. The poetry hero award here goes to poet and printmaker, Francesca Kay[17], who sells her haiku ingeniously in little packets like garden seeds.

"Lemon juice is fine on my avocado. I just don't eat vinegar." Is the sort of hipster problem overheard in the café, which incidentally serves a fabulous parsnip and apple soup drizzled with chilli oil. On the other hand it might be a dog day, when everyone with a dog is in here for coffee. Hay's shops are more than welcoming to our shaggy friends, which is entirely to be approved of. They are, after all no more unhygienic than many people, even

if not entirely friendly to all of their tribe, and thus completely like most people. There are some customers who tell themselves they will only stay as long as it takes to drink a cup of tea and so miss their lives while they are looking in quite the opposite direction. Stay a while and you can hear great music during the festivals, or learn to play poker, or, of course, attend the book club. And no-one minds if you plug in your mobile device and work or surf or whatever.

"HERE'S YOUR ARSENIC DEAR/ YOUR WEED KILLER BISCUIT"

So says Crippen-moustached Mr Pugh in *Under Milk Wood*[18] in his teasing fantasy of doing away with his nagging wife by means of her morning tea. There were several poisoners for Dylan Thomas to have modelled Mr Pugh on, and who knows, he may just have had Hay's infamous poisoner in mind. Bruce Chatwin certainly did as his character, Arkwright, the solicitor in *On the Black Hill* has been noted to have more than a passing resemblance to Major Herbert Rowse Armstrong.

Armstrong, a Hay solicitor, whose office was on Broad Street was hung in Gloucester Gaol in 1922, the only solicitor ever to meet this fate. The picture painted of this well-known, respectable citizen at his trial and by the attendant press is one of an archcriminal seeking to dispose with a rival, and rid himself of a troublesome wife in order to marry someone else. However more recent work by Martin Beales[19] vindicates him and points to a major miscarriage of justice. Beales' interest was piqued by reason of his not only practicing as a Hay solicitor himself in Armstrong's very office, but also living with his wife and family in Armstrong's house.

Armstrong came to the attention of the Home Office and police surveillance after one of his rival solicitors in town, Oswald Martin, fell ill with what the attending doctor, Hincks, diagnosed as arsenic poisoning. It was known that Martin and Armstrong, the more well-established of the two, were in discussions over some complex land transactions and were considered rivals. Armstrong was alleged to have poisoned Martin over afternoon tea at his large Victorian pile of a home, Mayfield (now The Mantles), in Cusop, involving possibly a deadly buttered scone. After this incident Hincks became concerned about the circumstances surrounding the death of Armstrong's wife, Katharine, which he had certified as due to heart disease. Her body was exhumed from St Mary's churchyard in Cusop and subjected to forensic testing. Arsenic was found and Armstrong was put on capital trial.

Beales' excellent book, *The Hay Poisoner*, on Armstrong's life and trial is a riveting read, and I don't even like crime stories that much, but I am interested in the workings of the law. What he does is lay out the facts from the trial, assess the evidence afresh, and evaluate the legal process itself. He finds all three things very much flawed and wanting. The forensic work on Katharine's body was highly unreliable given the time that had elapsed between her death and exhumation. The prosecution failed to establish the means by which Armstrong administered the poison. Yes, there was arsenic at Mayfield as it was used to mix up weedkiller by Armstrong, a very determined gardener. And there was undyed arsenic, undyed due to a chemist's error in dispensing it. As to motive, this was not properly established. There was no other woman in Armstrong's life in the sense that we would understand it, merely a family friend, who later might have become something more. Plus the judge, Justice Darling, who had a hanging reputation, asked a great number of questions himself, showed bias in demeaning the defence's expert witnesses, and over-rode the law in his expectation that the defence prove Armstrong did not do it as opposed to just the prosecution demonstrating beyond reasonable doubt that he did, and for allowing the Martin incident and Katharine's death to be linked and examined together.

So far, so bad, as Beales describes, and one might say the outcome was a foregone conclusion for poor Armstrong. Despite protesting his innocence all along, he was not helped by his own counsel's mis-steps. But what is the truth? Beales' theory is that there is sufficient medical and other evidence to show that Katharine either died of Addison's disease, or even committed suicide. He is convinced, and certainly convinced me that, despite the trial theatrics, including Armstrong's bureau being carried along the streets of Hereford to the Assizes, his children were illegally orphaned and an innocent man was sent to the gallows. Gloomy stuff indeed, but here's a random fun Hay fact: in the 1994 TV series, *Dandelion Dead*, based on the Armstrong case, the chemist's wife was played by Rhoda Lewis, whose son, Peter Florence and once an actor himself, founded the Hay Festival.

TELLING THE TIME

No-one in Hay needs to wear a watch. Ever. The Clock Tower is especially helpful to me as I seem to be one of those people whose magnetic field disrupts time keeping. That was something of a problem in my previous life where every six minutes of my time had to be accounted for and charged to a client code, as every watch I have ever owned broke inexplicably within a few months. The tower is an un-missable piece of Victorian gothic marking the end of Broad Street. In was commissioned in 1884 by the executors of one Captain Brown who had left a legacy for the installation of a clock on the church tower. Given that this is too far from the centre of town, the *twmpa*, or tump at the foot of Lion Street was chosen as the site for this extravagant piece of civic showing off.

It's tall, befitting a tower, and very fancy, just look at this description from Coflein, the organisation for the monuments of Wales[20]:

all square tower with chamfered angles; rubble with some freestone dressings. Pyramidal slate roof in 2 stages with open bellcote and weathervane; pyramidal roof lucarnes to each face. Moulded eaves with machicolations. Round clock faces to each side set in pointed arched frames with linked hoodmoulds and stringcourse. Scalloped corbels to angles with 3 treefoils between; 2 arrowslits to each face. Heraldic band with set-offs below and diagonal buttresses with punched treefoil gablets. Double cusped arched openings to N and S sides with hood mouldings and nook shafts; blocked to S boarded double doors to N.

If that doesn't sound like an ostentatious confection of architectural elements, then I'm stumped, and the poet in me really enjoys some of these compounded noun technical terms.

The clock has an unnecessarily loud chime on the quarters that can be heard a mile away, really, and right through the night, so all us insomniacs can count our hours with ease. These days it is annoyingly three minutes late and has a passive role in the life of Hay, strung with bunting during the summer months and presiding over part of the Thursday market. But during the police investigation of Armstrong in the 1920s, police constables apparently hid in the tower to stake out their subject's movements around town; a farcical scene with them, no doubt, unable to avoid the attentions of the feathered residents of the bellcote.

CHANCERY LANE – NEITHER A BORROWER OR A LENDER BE

Another day and after another delicious coffee at The Globe, I make my way up Chancery Lane to the Hay Library; a rather hideous grey brick affair from the '60s or '70s; the brutal decades. It's blockiness is softened by planting, including a huge rosa rugosa, bronze phormium, and variegated dark purple buddleia. Architecture aside, this important town asset is no more. Can you imagine, a book town without a library? How unthinkably ironic, yet the library closed to lenders in June 2018. Astonishing and disgraceful. And that was despite a huge campaign by HOWLS[21], the Hay-on-Wye Library Supporters, who raised objection after objection with Powys Council over a two year period.

Much is to be mourned here, not the least by writers like the local-ish Christopher Meredith[22] from Brecon, who wrote most of his first novel, *Shifts*, in Hay Library of an evening after work. The library moved to the newly rebuilt junior school off Oxford Road. It is not exactly accessible given its opening hours, which are just two hours of a morning three days a week, and four and a half hours on three afternoons a week, not necessarily the same days. It is closed all day on Tuesdays and Wednesdays. And, as I write, it is threatened with complete closure. Shame, in very large measure, on Powys Council for being yet another local authority responsible for closing libraries across the country. This modern day Beechingism makes me spitting mad. The importance of a library to any town or city should be self-evident, but in case it isn't, I recommend Jeannette Winterson[23] on the topic.

There is a glimmer of hope though, if and only if the town council can find the funds to keep it open. Not wanting to volunteer staff it, the council wants, quite rightly, to pay for a qualified librarian. In the meantime the council is scrabbling for support as it does not want to increase the precept it has to spend; an astonishingly small £8 per person per annum. Supported by donations on ticket bookings at the Hay Festival, a new CIC has been formed by HOWLS to apply for government grant money, or possible subscriptions to which the council can add funds. Local, national, international philanthropists, it's time to step up with large amounts of cash. Books everywhere in Hay, but none for the borrowing? No more infants' story time, no more internet access for those without computers, no quiet place to read? Unconscionable. Meanwhile, the good news is that click and collect and booking for in-person browsing continues as the pandemic winds on. But the less good news is that Powys County Council have not given up on closing the library. A 2021 'hands off' campaign to negotiate a five-year contract to keep it open is in progress. Fingers crossed for all the hard work being done on this.

NORTH

BRIDGE STREET AND NORTH – THE SYLVAN WYE

Hay was not known as Hay-on-Wye until 1947, not that anyone other than a total outsider would call it that. Ever. To ignore the river though is too much, so I am making my way out of town along Bridge Street, past a little row of houses one of whose occupants likes to dry their laundry by hanging it half out of an upstairs window; today, a pair of jeans and a grey t-shirt. To reach the river I'm ducking down via a little patch of park that contains one of the sculptures of the Via Beata[24]. Here, at the Hay way station on the pilgrim trail from Lowestoft to St Davids, the artwork is a stone and slate bench made by Will Spankie[25], which was installed in 2010. Spankie is a Hampshire-based sculptor of sinuous organic forms in stone and wood. He is also a stone letter carver. He exhibits all over the UK and has his public commissions can be found similarly. The bench carries the words from St John's gospel (Chapter 6 verse 68 to be precise): "Lord to whom shall we go? You have the words of eternal life" in both Welsh and English. The purpose of the sculpture trial, traversing the country via existing footpaths and rights of way, is to provide scripture for meditation along the journey. If one were to make it to St Davids and go there four times, it is the same as a pilgrimage to Rome. Or so I have it on the good authority of fellow poet and friend, the Dean of St Davids, – the long titled Reverend Canon Doctor Sarah Rowland-Jones. I should consider myself lucky and/or blessed then that I have been to both Rome and St Davids on multiple occasions. I don't have time to think about the quotation, not today, my focus is elsewhere.

The Wye lies north of Hay running east and north-east before it swings south from Witney and on to Hereford. Here it is a river in middle stage, gently meandering across its floodplain, sometimes making ox-bow lakes, as in the one in formation to the west of Hay towards Glasbury and which will silt up from the river to make a lake with an island at some point. In summer it is shallow and filled with islands of shingle where the water can no longer carry its load. These are stabilized by willows and other trees, and the water is full of long stranded weed like mermaids' hair. It's not exactly a pleasure to go canoeing at this time of the year as it's very easy to scrape the bottom of your boat on the gravels, which shift and change in the current. One might even come to a grinding halt, much to the entertainment of watchers from the bridge, if this is where misfortune strikes you. The slow curve of the river at The Warren allows for a pebble beach to form and that's definitely to be avoided in a boat, but not if you are looking for a good place to sunbathe on one of those rare hot summer's days, or are in search of a sunset viewing spot.

Writers have waxed rhapsodic about the Wye, and not necessarily at Hay. It has been variously described: "...again I hear / These waters, rolling from their mountain springs/ With a sweet inland murmur..."[26], which is a bit of a stretch even for Wordsworth as the Wye above Tintern, which he is thinking of in this poem, let alone at Hay, is quite a long way from its source, but poets, license!; and as "O sylvan Wye! Thou wanderer through the woods/ How often has my spirit turned to thee"[27], a sentiment, no doubt felt by both inhabitant and visitor in the years since Wordsworth made his Wye tour. Kilvert sees the river on an exquisitely clear day "like a silver serpent, flowing beneath at the foot of the poplars"[28]; and Bruce Chatwin calls it "a silver ribbon snaking through water meadows"[29], and so it is when looked down on from any nearby rise.

River Song

Take me back to the beginning:
to the slow welling of water
seeping from saturated rock,
filling the spring with life.

Rush me down the fast stream
through a steep valley,
picking up speed, stones
and deafening noise.

Swirl me in a helix,
carving meanders into horseshoes
and leaving oxbows to silt
in sedgy fields.

On the flatter plain
let me flood and retreat
in my ease, as the fancy takes me.
Let me mellow along.

Twice daily in the tideway,
mix me with brine
in the slow dance of ebb and flow,
marking waves in the mud flats.

Watch me letting go of years
of sediment in the estuary.
See me pick out new ways,
finally, to reach the sea.

In winter the Wye is another story. After heavy rain and in full spate, it is deep, turbulent and loaded with sediment from the surrounding hills and fields. Before the water control afforded by the Elan Valley reservoirs in mid-Wales in their two stages of building ending in 1904 and 1952 respectively, the Wye was prone to flash flooding and crossing it meant using either a ferry or a ford. The construction of the Elan Valley dams, which during the Second World War famously allowed Barnes Wallis a testing ground, or rather, water, for his bouncing bombs, is more than a sore point for the Welsh, involving as it did the destruction of local communities.

It has not been the only time part of Wales was sequestered to meet English needs as Tryweryn in North Wales in the 1960s attests, and which has not been forgotten. The 2019 campaign to remind everyone of it was prompted by damage done to its memorial graffiti. Now the familiar white lettering on a red ground, *Cofiwch Dryweryn* (Remember Tryweryn), first written by poet, Meic Stephens (1938-2018), has been daubed on hillsides and buildings around Wales recently. And that's not the end of the English using Wales for nefarious purposes, as seen for example the current dumping of nuclear mud from Hinkley Point power station in Gloucestershire into Cardiff Bay off Penarth. To me though, as a child bored on a long journey to Elan to see nothing more than a large body of water on a grey and, of course, rainy day, and being meant to marvel over it as an engineering feat, whilst simultaneously have a lecture on why the city of Birmingham should pay Wales for our water, was in truth, extremely dull.

The inconvenient village

If I didn't know, I'd admire the gasp of water;
reward for the car straining uphill and over
the old rock mountains of outcrop,
scree and violet summer heather,
past the lake made high in a valley.

If I didn't, I'd pause a while to catch breath
by the bracken and watch the wind
make patterns on the vast surface,

waves and ripples, white horses in gales,
the lake held by tons of stone.

As I can't un-know the tale of Tryweryn
despite its upland beauty, I feel the ancient anger:
my mother tapping the kitchen table
insistent, still, that Liverpool pays for our
water, whether it used or no.

    A bridge was built at Hay in 1763, but it and its successor were
swept away in heavy flooding. This explains the current elevated
and strong-piered bridge. It may not be pretty, and walking
underneath its concrete on the Bailey Walk footpath I could be in
any urban place, with some annoying graffiti, but minus the burnt
out shopping trolleys, drug dealers and the homeless, seeking
shelter, but it is above all things, practical. There are though still
floods in Hay, just not catastrophic enough to do away with the
bridge, yet. January and February 2020 are case in point as several
incidents of heavy rainfall swelled the Wye to bursting. The lower
path to The Warren and its cottage were flooded, along with
cottages near Dulas Brook, and cars left in the Gliss car park were
inundated with several being swept down river. Storms Ciara and
Dennis were to blame. Witness the effects of global warming, which
we are only beginning to recognise, let alone learn to live with.

The Wye rises on Plynlimon in mid Wales and flows for 152 miles. It is a Special Area of Conservation (SAC) under the EU Habitats directive. One way of judging the health of the river is to look at its salmon catches. The Wye is famous among fishermen as the finest river south of Scotland for Atlantic salmon. That will make it the best in both England and Wales then. The fish stock was in such abundance that anecdotally in the 1930s the people of Hay requested a halt to fishing as they were so fed up with eating salmon. Their petition requested that they not be expected to eat it more than three times a week. And it is for the salmon that banker, Benjamin Guinness bought Hay Castle in 1937. He used it as his fishing lodge before it was overtaken by a fire in 1939. There's a grand photograph from the early nineteenth century in Richard Booth's autobiography[30] showing one of his female relatives holding up a salmon on a pole. The fish is almost as large as she is tall and her elbows are wedged on her hips to help her bear its weight. No legend then. The fish in the Wye were giants.

Today, fish stocks on the river are healthy-ish and have recovered from their severe decline in the 1970s, '80s and '90s, yet a ten year mandatory catch and release byelaw operates on the Wye until 2022. This rather spoils the point of bothering to catch salmon, no? There speaks the non-sportswoman, who can only ever see fishing as the means to a meal. Perhaps I was spoiled in childhood by the cousins who had one of the few last fishing rights on a stretch of the Teifi in Ceredigion. Our going away present after a visit was always a magnificent and enormous shimmery fish.

The king of fish is just one of the species that contributed to the river's SAC classification. Others in this site that are most in need of conservation include: white-clawed crayfish, lampreys (all three kinds), the bottom dwelling bullhead, the ridiculously named Twaite shad, which is a member of the herring family, and not surprisingly with all these fish, the largest and densest population of otters in Wales. Some of the flora of note is straight from Harry Potter's Herbology book; water crowfoot, flowering rush, various of the ranunculus family, lesser water parsnip, curled pond weed, the rather vile looking river jelly lichen.

All this talk of river life is making me hungry. Of course, there are a gazillion ways to cook fish; the more sauced and added to, the more you are disguising the fact that the fish has been hanging around for a few days, has that cloudy-eyed look, and is less than fresh. Best avoid all of that and keep it as simple as possible to thoroughly enjoy the flavour. My favourite way with the freshest of trout, as an alternative to salmon, is to grab it from the nearest fisherman. So smile nicely at one of the chaps who spend their days flicking lines and fancy flies across the Wye. I then rush it to the tap to wash off the fine film that tells you it's just left the water. Next it needs to be gutted and gilled. Sharp knife only, and no squeamishness. This is not a recipe for people who are uncomfortable with the source of their food, who I advise to look away.

In case you don't know how to gut a fish, insert you knife point at its anus – the hole on its bottom side – and cut on this line right up to its gills. Remove all the blood and guts from inside, right back to the spine. You will need to get your hands dirty. If you can be bothered, also remove the gills. Rewash. You can trim the fins if you like and want to make eating the skin easy. These are best removed with a scissors.

Trout to hand, all you now have to do it fry it in a heavy pan in foamy Welsh butter till its skin is nice and golden brown and its flesh just cooked. Add a little seasoning, and perhaps a smidge of fresh herbs or a few almonds, if you must, and there it is, ready to be enjoyed with a green salad, good bread or a few minted new potatoes. Pimpsey.

from A Year of Fish
June

I lived once in a world of greens,
of reeds coiling, bending in the current,
of circles and duck weed floating above my head.

From my rock shelf I could reach out
and tickle those brilliant trout, those lozenges
refracting in the stream.

I could kiss them into a gentle trance.
Only when thrashing on the grass
did they realise it wasn't a dream.

Healthy though the river may have become, there are pollution incidents to be contended with, such as the one in July 2020 on the Llynfi, a tributary of the Wye that joins it at nearby Glasbury. The third such in recent years, it killed tens of thousands of fish and other species. And then there are the algae blooms, such as on the River Lugg that joins the Wye east of Hereford, apparently linked to chicken farming. They turn the river into a disgusting sludge of green slime choking its wildlife. Fines for breaches when the culprits are identified are all very well, but you can't revivify the devastated plant and animal communities with money.

OFFA'S DYKE PATH

Taking a detour on the way to Clyro, the small village that is one mile to the north of Hay, I turn right after Hay bridge and down onto one of two sections of the Offa's Dyke Path that runs through Hay. The other leads south out over the fields towards the Beacons starting from south of the main town car park on Oxford Road. The path is one of our glorious long distance footpaths, or National Trails, in this case mostly following the ancient earthworks of bank and ditch built by King Offa of Mercia in the eighth century, and for much of its route marking the Anglo-Welsh border. There are no earthworks at Hay though. To see those nearest involves a trip some twenty-three miles north to Knighton, where the dyke has its own visitor centre[31]. This charity is worth your membership or donation as it lost its funding from Powys County Council in 2017 and survives now on the largesse of the visiting public. At about the halfway mark along the trail, the centre has exhibits on the construction of the dyke, Anglo-Saxon history, and the local environment. Before we walk here's a fun fact about Offa's wife, Cynthryth: she was the only Anglo-Saxon queen in whose name coinage was issued – so she must have been rather powerful in her own right, methinks.

The path crosses the border some twenty times along its route from Chepstow in the south to Prestatyn in the north. It's a good thing that I am walking it today and not in earlier times, when folklore has it that is was customary for the English to cut off the ears of any Welshman found east of the dyke, and for the Welsh to hang any Englishmen found to its west. Dangerous place, this border, if you believe the kind of fanciful 'keep out' hyperbole reported in the nineteenth century[32]. Absent dyke notwithstanding, the path is a pleasant stroll out of Hay along the northern bank of the Wye, whose song is accompaniment past rape fields, sheep and hay meadows. It turns north through a field of wheat and between two hedgerows until it meets the main road. Hundreds of people walk the path every year in one go, camping along the way, or in sections, or on one of the suggested circular walks. I meet plenty of rather fit, but not always young people taking up this challenge as they pass through Hay, or if they stop to camp in the same field as me. I am always in admiration of their dedication and perseverance.

The trail is renowned for its stunning landscapes and the historical sites that are either on it or very close by. There are castles, churches and hill forts to enjoy. If dusty history is not your thing, then how about some technology to play with? The path has a number of geo-caches for you to find. Geo-caching? No, me neither, but my children tell me this is the cool way to explore a new place. All you need is the GPS on your phone and the downloaded App[33] and you can start searching for hidden items in specially marked boxes and containers – they could be anything and you can even do swapsies – almost wherever you are in the world. There are over three million caches, including virtual ones, as I write and there are several hidden by members of the caching community on the Offa's Dyke Path. Looking for them in this high-tech treasure hunt and logging your visit will take you to some of the best views. Oh and there is actual treasure to be found on the trail in the form of geo-coins, minted annually at the start of the July holidays. If you find one of these beauties it might ask you to take it to another of the National Trails, or pass it along the home trail. That will be your mission. Fun, no? It certainly beats wrestling map and compass on one of too many geography field trips in the driving wind and rain.

Not wanting to do much more of the path's one hundred and seventy-seven miles, I turn back and retrace my steps, making for the mixed oak woodland. A soft wind is rustling the tree branches, but I'm thinking about dog poo. Here, and along the southerly bank of the Wye, and along The Warren, and well, all over Hay, there are dog walkers who just don't scoop. This causes much consternation, and a lot of moaning and naming and shaming on the Hay Community Facebook page. The council have even taken to spraying the offending deposits with orange paint. Quite why, no-one is sure: as a warning, or in admonition? No, it's more practical than that: it's so the Woodland Group volunteers won't step in the stuff when they are busy working on the paths. The plea is always to pick up the damn poop. I rummage for a degradable bag and do the decent thing. Oh, and I don't leave the bag as some kind of way marker protest. I do actually put it in the marked bin.

WALKING THE WYE VALLEY

Another day, another footpath, another way to enjoy the beauty of the Welsh landscape, and you can even have your luggage hauled for you along the Wye Valley Walk by the Hay taxi service as you do so. From Plynlimon to the sea – source to mouth – some of the one hundred and thirty-six miles of this long distance footpath are through Hay. Mostly following existing rights of way, there are some permissive paths allowed by the generosity of landowners, as well as vast sections of unfettered access on the Plynlimon Massif. The right to roam there and elsewhere was granted by the Countryside Right of Way Act of 2000; a fitting piece of legislation enacted nearly eighty years after the mass trespass on Kinder Scout by ramblers in 1932. Chapeau to them all for starting the process that has secured our rights to wander, run, climb and

watch the wildlife in the now designated open country of mountain, moorland, heathland and downland, and, if we want to, get thoroughly lost.

East to west the walk crosses the Wye at Bredwardine, but strays away from the river for much of its path, only getting close to it before Clifford and as it crosses the river at Hay Bridge. Striking west from Hay, the walk follows the bends and meanders of the Wye until it crosses the main road at Llowes. Rejoining the

river at Glasbury, the path follows the Wye north to Builth Wells. Some say it's a gentle and less demanding trail than the Offa's Dyke Path, and certainly it is shorter, but I don't know, any footpath in Wales is going to be a two week challenge of hill, stone and mud. The added benefit of this one is the spectacular waters of the Wye chanting in accompaniment to one's footsteps.

The section immediately west from Racquety Farm, which is where you turn off from the Clyro road to access it, leads you past the fine stone walls that border the farmhouse garden and down into a bluebell wood. There's a convenient fallen log with an invitation to take a seat, but this is too soon into the walk to be doing any sitting down. Out from the wood and towards the river then, you follow the water upstream on the small river cliffs. Fields of eye-burning rape and winter wheat are your accompaniment in spring. The hawthorn is brilliant this year in its bridal white, and every apple tree in the world is in full pink blossom. The distant blue-black mountain that seems to be drawing me on with its distinct outline is Pen y Fan near Brecon; the highest point of the Beacons, all eight hundred and eighty-six metres of it, and a pretty tough ascent, I can tell you. On this particular afternoon, I am buoyed along by a pair of swans, which make swimming upriver look like nothing, even though the flow is pacey. Birdsong from a myriad of members of the thrush family, and sheep bleating from somewhere unseen, make for the soundtrack. I get carried away and walk far too far, twice, as I have to a retrace my steps. Later I spot one of the swans in flight over the river. Even from some distance the thud of its wing beats is surprisingly loud, and in this watching I spot my first swallows of the year. Joy.

I had wanted to make it as far as Glasbury, some four or so miles from Hay and a eight mile round trip, but I underestimate both the length of the path on the ground and the ability of my arthritic knees to walk it. The destination was meant to be the splendid ox-bow lake, or a geographical process in action. These features are part of the wandering progress of a river and they don't last long in geological time, as eventually they drain away and fill with bog-loving vegetation. They are not rare, but they're not common either given our habit of over-managing rivers. Pity I missed this literal geo-cache.

DIG IT

Not quite halfway to Clyro, Ros and Geoff Garratt have run Racquety Farm, organically, for decades. I glamp in their fields in the summer months, grateful that apart from my tiny tent and duvet I do not have to bring a plethora of camping equipment with me as the outdoor kitchen is fully equipped. Luxuriously supplied by microwave, kettle and all the pots and dishes one could want, along with the most important thing, a decent hot shower, I can sit back and enjoy the unparalled views of Hay, the castle and the hills and mountains beyond. And when the fancy takes me, kick about the fields in the footsteps of hunting cats, although I'm usually looking for flowers not voles.

The good thing about glamping is that it's camping for softies, hence the unparallelled luxury of a duvet and a soft pillow, and I don't even need to rough it as far as a having a tent if I don't want to. The campsite offers the option of geodesic domes with actual beds, and even a shepherd's hut from which one gets the benefit of being close to nature without the bad back from sleeping on the ground for four nights. So there's really no excuse to not get out there and listen to the birds, or fall asleep of an afternoon under the linden tree, whose blossom is a known somnifer. Radios and late night noise are banned, after all no-one likes other people's soundtracks while we are trying to look at the stars. If you come at festival time, the farm will be chock-a-block with tents and temporary yurts, but that's how to make friends with people with whom you will have at least one thing in common; a love of books.

Part of one of the farm's lower fields towards the river was set aside in 2010 and rented out as Hayfield Community Garden, which is one of the projects of Hay as a transition town[34]. The transition movement started in 2005 with the aim of, amongst other things, developing grass roots community-based local economies worldwide, uncoupling from a reliance on multi-nationals and big oil. It is self-sufficiency for the new millennium and attractive to me as a concept as I am the child of a quasi-self-sufficient father who grew most of our vegetables and bred rabbits for the pot. As a teenager in the 1970s, I kept bees in the city before it was *de rigeur* to do so, and one of my bedside books was John Seymour's *Self-Sufficiency*.

The garden is laid out as a large allotment for growing all the

vegetables you can think of, and there is a geodesic dome to extend their seasons. The principles here are organic and permaculture. Those who work the land enjoy its bounty. The crops are looking good this summer, but there is much grass and areas of wild. I imagine these are deliberate to encourage wildlife. Despite Ros' worries that it is a bad butterfly year, I saw a beauty in orange with brown speckles by the compost bins, but that might be me mistaking weather changes for climate ones, a school girl error. The plum tree is laden, heavy with fruit; give it a few weeks. The PYO raspberry sign has been taken down and is stored behind the geodome. The commercial season is over, although there are enough jewelled fruits on the first rows of canes for several bowlfuls still. I sneak a few handfuls of sweetness and make a note to come back in a few weeks for the bounty of the autumn fruiting variety.

Saturday afternoon, yet no-one is tending the garden. Eat Together instructs the paint-chipped Timbuktu trail sign. Today that must mean strawberries and cream in front of the Wimbledon ladies final. Shouts from canoe enthusiasts ring over the field from the river. The water is low and they are getting stuck on the gravels and in the weed. The bikers who passed me on their Harleys are boozing in the Three Tuns. Ah summer. Ah Hay.

How to garden[35]

There's something curious
in knowing how to garden
by the phases of the moon,

how to plant seeds at the moment
when the soil is just so warm,
has most moisture.

So I buy moon charts, look
for times when the sea is tranquil,
plan the year out on the tides,

but one night I mistake the hour
and flounder about in the dark
planting snowdrops.

CLYRO

Just one mile north of Hay, the village of Clyro is bisected by the
A438, which is a real pity as it rather spoils the place, making it
not only difficult for the residents from the south of the road to
cross to the centre of the village on the other side, but noisy from
the traffic to boot. A mixture of mainly Victorian houses cluster
around the church and the whole is tucked under a hill, from
which, if you climb it, there is a splendid view of the Beacons. So
much for ancient tourist guide speak.

BUT A THROW AWAY

Doing Kilvert in reverse means walking from Hay to Clyro, the
tiny place for whom he is its claim to fame. He often mentions his
walk across the fields to town, but as there isn't a clear footpath in
the direction I want to travel, and I am not one for roaming across
land unbidden, I am walking along the road. It's uphill, more of a
hill than you notice when you are speeding along in a car. And it
seems that everyone speeds on this section of road. Not that there

is a huge amount of traffic, mind you, but it's enough to make my rather nervous dog, jump into the hedge periodically. The blackberries are in full fruit. Their harvest has been amazing this year. We must have had just the right combination of sun and late summer rain. I have made pounds of jam and frozen bags of fruit, not that I am going collect any from the roadside, now. There is too much chance of pollution from cars and passing canines. The birds can have these ones.

The first place of note as I arrive in Clyro is Pottery Cottage. Now a well-appointed holiday let – I know as I've stayed there – it was the studio of Adam Dworski, a noted potter. Dworski arrived in Wales in 1956 and worked here for some forty years before moving to France in the final years of his life. Born in what is now Croatia and what was then Austria-Hungary in 1917, he came to the UK when he married his British wife, Patricia, in 1954. The Wye Pottery and Dworski became well known: his work can be found in private collections, and those of Warwick University, for example. Two of his works were commissioned for the new Coventry Cathedral, and Loretta Scott-King had one of his black Madonnas. Dworski's work encompassed wheel thrown domestic wares, as well as figures and highly coloured plaques reminiscent of stained glass windows. Some of these were cemented into the render of the cottage and remain to this day as evidence of the cottage's name. The centenary of his birth was celebrated in 2017

with an exhibition of over a hundred loaned pieces, and a commemorative book by artist and writer Graham Hobbs, who lives in the village. My own piece of Dworski's work is a smallish swirly patterned bowl in subtle greens and greys that I frequently use for everything from pasta to fruit. It's a beauty to behold.

DECORATING THE GOTHIC

Crossing the busy road and into the main part of Clyro, it's time to see what puts this tiny place on the map, namely St Michael and All Angels' church[36], to give its full title. Workplace of curate and diarist, Francis Kilvert, and parish church of lords of the manor, the Baskerville family, it is right in the centre of the village. The red and yellow sandstone church squats in its grassy yard at the foot of a small hill and has a few things to say for itself. It's a Victorian rebuild, in 1853, of the previous twelfth century church and thus an extended improvement on the gothic. Its square tower seems to have ancient stones in its mix, and its crenellated top and thin windows make it look for all the world like a Norman defensive structure. Its clock was a gift in 1894 from the Baskervilles. The interior is rather unexciting, apart from its box pews, and lovely mediaeval stone piscina, the basin for washing

the communion vessels. It's a quiet spot to pause and wonder, as I often do looking up at the ribbing of wooden rafters. Upturned boat, or skeleton of a whale? Either image will serve well for the monumental.

As well as the various plaques to the Baskervilles, there is also Kilvert's plaque, noting his good and faithful service. Kilvert was born at Hardenhuish, near Chippenham in Wiltshire in 1840, son of rector Robert Kilvert. He was educated at home and graduated from Wadham College, Oxford and then entered the Church. His second curacy was at Clyro, where he arrived in 1865. From 1872 to 1876 he was curate to his father at Langley Burrell, near Chippenham. In 1877 he returned to these parts to become vicar at Bredwardine. Between 1870 and 1879 he kept his diary of country life, which is considered a minor classic of Victorian literature in which, for all his gentility, Kilvert does not hesitate to make his opinions clear.

A photograph of him in St Michael's reveals a youngish man with full beard, the kind that wouldn't look out of place these days on your average hipster. It is sobering to consider his dates, 1840-1879, a mere thirty-nine years. No time at all before he died of peritonitis just weeks after his marriage to Elizabeth Rowland. Thankfully, though we have his thoroughly enjoyable diary, or at

least those selected extracts from it that have found their way into print. Kilvert's home in the village is actually a rather large house by today's standards. The life of the Victorian curate can't have been half bad if this was part of his living. The house is noted by a plaque and easy to find – there few streets to walk in Clyro. I imagine its present owners are tolerant of curious passers-by with cameras. There aren't that many of us, after all.

BASKERVILLE HALL AND A VERY BAD MARKETING DECISION

Coming west from Clyro, I am turning off from the main Brecon Road and walking up the long wooded drive of the Baskerville Hall Hotel. It is spring and daffodils are nodding their custard trumpets across the entire land. Here they are grouped in so many large clumps under the trees as to make a sea of yellow dancers that will no doubt later "flash upon that inward eye"[37], but this is no time for going all Romantic. The driveway is befittingly long, National Trust long. I should have driven, but the day is sunny and I need the exercise. Finally I make it to the Hall, a huge early Victorian mock-Jacobean pile and large gentleman's residence, built in the middle of over a hundred acres by Sir Thomas Mynors Baskerville in 1839. Its mellow, now darkening stone, imposing size and, of course, that name, have me slightly worried, even in the daytime.

The Hall is an hotel now and not a super-luxurious one. Despite its grand stone and iron staircase that sweeps up and divides itself onto the first floor, and its elaborate marble fireplaces, it suffers from some pretty hideous rear extensions. They look like they were built in the 1970s, prompting the question as to how on earth they were given planning permission, so rectangular, partially wood-cladded and functional as they are. The answer surely lies in the hotel's one time incarnation as a school. Now in some state of disrepair, they give the whole place an air of decrepitude. Couple this with the less than lovely garden and the predictable howling wolf-dog carved, badly, from the trunk of a dead tree at the edge of the long south-facing lawn and I am no longer worried, rather disappointed. I expected more.

Sir Thomas Baskerville, the Conservative MP for Herefordshire from 1841 to 1850, built the Hall for his second wife, Elizabeth Guise, who he married in 1836. With a lineage tracing back to the Norman conquerors, he was a man of standing in public service. As well as being an MP, he was a Deputy Lieutenant, the High Sheriff of Wiltshire in 1827, and a Justice of the Peace, and he was generous to boot, being, for example, one to the subscribers for the sum of ten guineas to the Royal Horticultural Society's Chiswick garden in 1824. This brings him, more or less, to my London door, albeit more than half a century before that door was built.

His heraldic shield is something to behold: divided into sixty quarterings, it is surmounted by a fiercesome and hirsute wolf-dog (it could be a hairy dragon, but let's not quibble) holding a blood dripping spear in its mouth, which takes us to the obvious. Sir Arthur Conan Doyle was a friend of the later Baskerville family and it is said he was a frequent visitor to the Hall, hence the adoption of the family name in that famous book of his. More than this name, the novel borrows the legend of the black dog, a possible manifestation of Black Vaughan, which roamed nearby Hergest Ridge. What legend?

One Sir Thomas Vaughan found himself on the wrong side in the Wars of the Roses and was beheaded at Banbury in 1469. His headless body is buried an elaborate tomb in Kington in Herefordshire, a few miles to the north east of Hay, and legend has it that his restless spirit took various forms (a fly on horses, a black dog, a black bull and so on) to wreak havoc on the local townsfolk, frightening ladies in coaches and the like. Subject to an exorcism, his spirit was allegedly funnelled into a snuff box and buried under a stone in Hergest Pool. But subsequent generations of the Vaughan family at Hergest Court reported being haunted by a black dog as the precursor to a death, according to historian Anne O'Brien[38], who notes that Conan Doyle is also known to have stayed at the Court.

Thus, from this mesh of possibilities it seems that the environs of Hay can lay good claim to being at least one of the sources of Conan Doyle's story. If that is true, explain then please why the novel is set on Dartmoor? Ah, well, like Wordsworth bemoaning the prospect of the railway bringing too many visitors to his beloved Lake District, in what might be seen now as a very bad marketing decision, the Baskervilles apparently asked Conan Doyle not to set the book around Clyro so as to prevent hoards of curious tourists knocking on their door, or like me, poking around the place uninvited. This was a rather ironic decision when viewed with today's hindsight, as a couple of miles away is book lovers central, and because the Hotel and the pub in Clyro, which decades ago changed its name from The Swan, as it was known in Kilvert's time, to the Baskerville Arms, might have had even more business from the Conan Doyle connection.

CENTRAL

TOWN HALL

Who'd want to govern Hay? Well, thankfully the excellent council and Mayor, Trudy Stedman, all unpaid, do their best to please as many of the people as they can at one time. The council offices are housed in a large Victorian building on the square behind the Clock Tower. When I say offices, I mean an office and the light oak panelled and tabled council chamber, as the rest of the building is given over to small businesses and charities, whose rent pays for the council's occupation. And even that is insufficient, as Powys County Council has determined that the building will be sold off in the very near future. Thus Hay, that huge player on the world's cultural stage, will not only not have a community centre, or a youth club, there will be nowhere for its hard-working council to work and meet. What is going on in this country right now? And lo, it came to pass. The building by the Clock Tower was sold and is being converted into a private dwelling as I write. The town council is relegated to an office in the Brecon Road Sports Centre.

You might consider that some of the issues the council grapples with are small scale and inconsequential, but I would disagree. Take the closure of the library for example, and the latest in a long list of things under threat: the closure of all the public conveniences in Hay. Not primarily for residents, but rather handy for visitors, I can attest, Powys wants them gone. The pennies paid – twenty in this case – are insufficient to cover the running costs and Powys are not prepared to pay the £10-12,000 per annum to make them break even. What to do? It looks like price increases and requests for business subsidies are the way forward if we don't all want to get caught short.

High on the list of priorities is dealing with the climate crisis. The council has declared a climate emergency and with funds from National Resources Wales is undertaking a number of projects in the town, involving, of course, its climate striking students, Low Carbon Hay, and Plastic Free Hay. With a six month action plan, as Trudy Stedman explains, it's the little things that add up, such as, looking at providing electric car charging points of which there were none until one was opened at Drover Cycles on Forest Road, and providing education and information to individuals and businesses.

Other projects that the council is presently working on to make this lovely place even more lovely include participating in Britain in Bloom. Hay has always had a well-planted horse trough at the junction of Bridge Street and Broad Street, but this competition is a step beyond that, and includes prizes primarily for business, but also for residents. It's all part of the greening of Hay and commendable just the same. Recognising people's contribution to the town is the remit of the Citizen of the Year Award, inaugurated in 2018 and made every April. Most recently it was given to Kelvyn Jenkins for his work in organising the First World War commemorations. The 2020 award was, of course, delayed, and at the time of writing has yet to be announced over a year later.

THE PAVEMENT – UNIQUE, AND YES, THE ONLY ONE IN THE WHOLE COUNTRY

A couple of shops up The Pavement from the Clock Tower and I am outside The Poetry Bookshop, newly painted in classy black, its huge Victorian windows crammed with the kind of treasure poetry readers can only dream of: from first editions of Bishop and Hughes, whose signature is now worth £350, to pamphlets, posters, and all kinds of interesting printed poetry matter. I start to salivate, push the door and enter the kingdom of the best words in the best order.

Chris and Melanie Prince moved their vast stock of poetry volumes to this more prominent location in 2017. For a decade or more poetry was squeezed into the ground floor of their stone-built house, slightly off the book browsers' beaten track in Brook Street. One definitely had to know it was there. A visit could take several hours, largely because I'd rummage for books of essays on poetry, not trusting myself not to buy duplicates of collections I already have, or I'd descend into the cold of the cellar's ice house in search of less popular items. I'd chat to Chris about poetry, how he loves to spend his days surrounded by these books, or about bookselling and the sad state of the trade.

People tell me they enjoy poetry readings, open mic, and spoken word events. They are a cheap and entertaining night out – cheap, because they are often free, as it seems us poets don't deserve to be paid. Similarly poetry on the radio is popular, but not many people actually buy actual poetry books – as the editor of this series will attest, having written three of its books all bemoaning this eternal fact – not even necessarily at readings, which is rather the point. I mean, when did you last do that, if ever? Thus poetry publishing and bookselling is a minority sport, one that I have spent most of my adult life playing, but one where people expect too much for nothing. I have been asked to travel half the country at my own expense to provide free entertainment in the form of a reading on the vague off chance that I might sell a couple of books. Not surprisingly, I generally turn down these tempting offers to make more of a loss from my rather expensive vocation.

When did we start disvaluing our writers so thoroughly? I recall the end of one reading when a nice lady complimented me on my work, said she had really enjoyed it very much, and then asked me where she could get it. I pointed to the book table, where three of my books were for sale. She scoffed and said, "No, no. I meant, where can I get it for free, on the internet?" Sigh. But this is the answer, the internet, for all its, many virtues, has distilled in us the notion that literature is free and writers live on thin air. I wish I had been quicker on that occasion to ask her whether she felt that she could just walk into an art gallery and help herself to whatever she fancied. But honestly, the cheek of it. And so bare-faced. And to my actual face!

Despite this kind of expectation, brave poetry publishers struggle on, brave poets work hard to see their work in print, and brave booksellers try to get the public to buy it. Many thanks if you do. Hurrah then for a world in which Chris and Melanie's beautiful new shop exists and where they somehow manage to carry on spreading our words. The only poetry bookshop in the U.K. is a little haven of sanity where you can trawl the vast shelves in peace, or attend the occasional reading by festival and other poets. Pick a book at random by a poet you've never heard of, read a poem and be transported. Better still take said book to the till and buy it, but don't for one minute think you can make an offer or ask for a discount on a secondhand book. All the world is not a bargain. Everything is not a deal. The books are fairly priced and the Princes have to live. One chap tried that in my hearing once, and was turned down very politely. What bad manners! He wouldn't do that in Hatchards.

Set the dogs on him, I say, or better still, a bear. This is not exactly a far-fetched idea, as somewhere under the shops of The Pavement there is a bear pit. Up until the early years of the twentieth century a cellar hereabouts was used to house the bears that were made to dance in the Bull Ring alongside the fun-fair rides and booths at the May and November hiring fairs. There's a poem there, when I get around to writing it.

LION STREET – WHERE IT ALL STARTED, ALMOST

Up Lion Street and I continue my book tour at the remaining place in Hay that still bears the book town founder's name: Richard Booth Books, not of course that the man himself owns the former merchant's store any more. Down from Oxford, Booth came to Hay in 1961 after his well-to-do parents moved to a grand house close by in Cusop Dingle. The boy who'd like me spent his childhood in second hand bookshops, opened his own and first in the Old Fire Station on Castle Street[39]. Over the succeeding years

and with various degrees of success and failure, riches and bankruptcy, he opened further shops in the Castle, on Castle Street, and at the Cinema (where for a year Booth held the Guinness Book of Records record for the largest second hand bookshop in the world with 250,000 books), and inventing along the way the idea of the honesty bookshop. This still exists in the Castle Yard and variously over the years has seen bookshelves pretty much open to the elements tucked under the low castle walls, in an old farm cart, or as today, under cover besides the high wall that divides the castle from its street. Like the idea of a book town, the honesty bookshop has been copied the world over.

Booth is considered a man of vision and courage, able to express his love/hate relationship with quangos – the agencies of Welsh tourism and development – and their misguided ideas and lack of democratic accountability. Booth was a constant critic of those who give tourism an economic role in rural areas like Hay beyond what is capable of being fulfilled, and whose grants are counter- productive, even though Hay was the fastest growing tourist place in the country. He even wrote a booklet on the subject in 1978 called *Abolish the Welsh Tourist Board.*

Booth's view is that the book town economy, growing as it has from agricultural depression and even desperation, has to be protected not subsidised, and that investment creates jobs. Hence his opposition to supermarkets and the like as they discourage visitors who come in search of what they cannot get at home. The book town economy thrives not because of the sale of second hand books, which after all make some, but really very little money, but because it is a tourist economy with visitors spending a great deal on accommodation, food and drink, in order to visit it. This is the concept, and by visiting a book town one is supporting an otherwise at risk rural economy. For a proponent of anarchy and chaos, Booth can sometimes sound pretty right wing to my ears. Perhaps that it is one of his charming contradictions.

To promote Hay and its businesses, Booth staged the kind of publicity coups that brought him into conflict with his neighbours, culminating in crowning himself the King of Hay, Richard I, Coeur des Livres, and declaring the old lands of Hay castle as independent from the UK on 1 April 1977. This was year of the Queen's silver jubilee, when poking fun at the monarchy with various degrees of viciousness was in certain quarters the fashion. If you are my age, you may recall a certain era-defining song by the Sex Pistols on this topic. 'God Save the Queen' and the album it came from, *Anarchy in the UK*, got me into a great deal of trouble with my parents. If I played it at all at home, it was when they were out, and it was the time when I realised that parents in general and mine in particular, just didn't get it.

Certainly a marketing stunt with the kingdom's own flag, and Booth's homemade regal paraphernalia – his travelling crown was a tea cosy, his orb a ball cock and his robes held together with safety pins (how punk!) – the declaration of independence had the desired effect of attracting nationwide publicity, annoying people – was he taking the piss out of Welsh devolution? and anyway who did he think he was – and drawing the curious book lover into town. A quick search on You Tube will find plenty of film footage of hilariously pomp-filled investitures, beatifications and the like with brass bands and military guards. There is even a documentary fairy tale called *Borderline*. Surprisingly enough, and displaying a total lack of ability to spot a satire, some local councillors took Hay's independence seriously, even issuing legal corrections of the constitutional position. To some, Booth was a danger.

Reading about it now, there is still a frisson in the semi-serious political messages of the independence campaign: one headline focuses on Hay quitting the European Economic Community (the precursor of the European Union) – oh, the present irony, and a campaign slogan 'Father died of Mother's Pride' attacks factory-produced nutritionally-absent food, while the booklet, *Independence for Hay*, criticises the local council, bemoans the closure of small shops and the railway, and advocates locally produced food and craft products. The kind of things that I for one value today and that are now available in abundance in Hay's market, speciality shops and galleries.

Hay and Booth were written about in the local and national press and there were even articles in prominent US papers. By 1976 ITN had given Hay a three minute slot and the town received £50,000 from the Welsh Tourist Board to help celebrate the bi-centenary of American Independence. Booth hastily created a bookshop with 80,000 American titles and hosted the US Ambassador in a bid to attract American tourists. The remnants of Booth's reign were still be found until 2018 in the King of Hay bookshop on Castle Street, where for a modest outlay one could purchase one's own Hay passport, inevitably stamped April 1st. In the past there was even edible currency, Hay stamps, and Dukedom's for sale. All pretty witty. And independence is still celebrated in one form or another in Hay today. 2019 was the third year of Hay Independence and Bookstagram festival; a week-long series of book related events. Dukedoms and Earldoms can still be acquired from the Hay Castle Trust.

Joking aside Booth had a serious intent, which he relates in his very entertaining autobiography, *My Kingdom of Books*[40]. As he explains: "The first Welsh books were published in Newcastle Emlyn, Trefecca and Carmarthen and were never much thicker than a lady's cigarette case. I like to think of Hay on Wye as part of a Welsh tradition because it is only a few miles from Trefecca, where followers of John Wesley produced some of the most beautiful publishing of the eighteenth century". Although commercial in his focus ("you can always sell a good book"), he did acquire huge numbers of historically important books and collections, preventing them from being lost or thrown away. Instead he supplied the burgeoning new universities the world over, specialist collectors, and the general book buyer – people like me who think life is complete curled up with a printed companion and a cuppa.

In terms of scale, we are talking millions of books, whole libraries full and not just from the UK, as Booth travelled to Ireland and the US in search of stock. As the shop's storefront still says, Books Bought Anywhere in the World. It's hard to envisage containers and lorry loads of books arriving in Hay, but that is how it was. And it was all manual labour. Auction houses like Sothebys were not interested in dealing with all these books, so Booth and his staff took on the mammoth task of sorting the tons of sheep from the tons of goats – as Booth says, the only commodity that is available in bulk to be sold in a rural area. Plenty of surplus and

damaged books may have eventually been burned or put in a landfill, but many treasures were saved to have a new life in the second hand book market.

That is what Hay's bookshops are all about. Booth describes his notion of a book town in terms of a mother bookshop with more specialised bookshops around it, and emphasises the need to create an international trade. Thus in Hay there are bookshops specialising in crime and detectives, children's books, Dickens and his contemporaries, and in the past there was a gardens and gardening bookshop. He was an opponent of new book selling in a book town as this is not what such places are all about, so I've no idea what he would make of his namesake shop currently, which has partly crossed to this dark side.

Richard Booth sadly passed way in August 2019, just as I was finishing this manuscript. The next day The Story of Books letter press had printed two mourning cards saying: 'Richard Booth, The King of Hay, 1938-2019, R.I.P.' and 'The King is Dead, Long Live the Kingdom! Hay-on-Wye'. Many of the bookshop windows in Hay sported these. Addyman's arranged its widows with black covered books of all genres. So, the end of an era. All good things. And all that. Everyone had their own Booth story to tell. One of my favourites was from an ex-employee who explained that Booth was often evasive and unclear, but somewhere in his highly creative ramblings were instructions; you just had to know when to listen and when to switch off. There was much talk and

speculation of how to memorialise Booth, not only on the afternoon of his funeral, when a procession was arranged from the centre of Hay to the church in Cusop and an evening gathering was held at The Globe, but also more permanently. Within days plans were afoot for an annual memorial day on 31 October with speeches, processions and much merriment, deferred now until after the pandemic. The spirit of independent Hay and the book town's founder is not going to go away any time soon. We can all rest assured of that. After all without him Hay would still be a nothing much place; just a windy street and a market. A place where, someone else told me, that if you were on the bus from Brecon, you would not want to alight.

Richard Booth's bookshop has been owned since 2011 by Elizabeth Haycox and her husband, who rescued the largely uneconomic business and has turned it rather splendidly and with much enthusiasm and energy into something else. American by birth, Haycox comes from a good pedigree of writing too as her grandfather, Ernest Haycox, is considered one of the top Western writers and was admired by both Stein and Hemingway. One of his three hundred or more short stories became *Stagecoach*, the 1939 film directed by John Ford that propelled John Wayne to Hollywood stardom.

Stepping over the bookshop threshold now, I am struck by the changes that have taken place during Haycox's tenure. The closed-in staircase has been opened out into its wide glory with art on the wall, and the shop seems more spacious and clean. It smells of wood polish. The dark bookshelves and pews are the same, but there are plenty of battered leather armchairs and squishy sofas for customers to use. The old school chairs still have the potential to snag tights and teach teenage-me a lesson in how to stop a run with nail varnish. The roof skylights still fill the first floor with light, even on a typically cloudy Welsh day. It is inviting, yes and there are even chairs in the front window for the serious book poseur to pretend to read in, but it's lost a little something of the old, dusty musty chaos and magic. The heart of Hay has been given a transplant. It's not like your average branch of Waterstones, but it's close, and that's not just because of the new books. It might be because there is now a café, and close by a yoga studio and a cinema.

Care is needed with these kinds of gentrifications so as not to kill the brand, the very thing that made it unique in the first place. Richard Booth is no longer there to sign each book with his extravagant signature, a flourish on each front page, so I shall hold tight to those that I own bearing this trademark. The hugely popular café is almost too nice with its waitress service and waiting to be seated, and as I sip a rather good cup of coffee and note the topiaried box on the terrace, I am half-mourning the end of an era. Reassuring overhearings though keep me buoyed: "How many books can I take home?", "Well, you've got an estate car, so no more than you can fit in that".

A cinema in the middle of nowhere? What a marvel! Many people are very, very happy about this. Its feature stonewalls and comfy chairs are a great addition to Hay and its one carefully chosen film a week might also be a theatre performance from London, a truly wonderful phenomenon. As for being allowed to bring a glass of wine into the auditorium, well, there's nothing more civilised in my book. Upstairs are kilim-strewn ottomans for pre or post screening socialising, making for a sumptuous and upmarket affair, which at £9 a ticket is a bargain compared to the Curzons and Everymans in London.

THINGS YOU BELIEVE TO BE BEAUTIFUL

Out from Booth's, I backtrack a little to The Table. This is a combination of art gallery and restaurant run by Val Harris. Its changing exhibitions are fascinating in themselves, and as a backdrop for a delicious Sunday lunch served on the room long trestle table, are a delight. There's nothing offensive or especially challenging about the art Val choses to show, and that's the point, gentle, subtle and beautifully made work that I'd be happy to look at every day on my own walls.

I must pinch myself as I've managed to write a whole paragraph about art without using the word curate. I'm on a campaign against this much inappropriately overused term. In an art context, of course, it is entirely correct, but not anywhere else. I am fed up of reading about a carefully curated selection of artisanal coffees, cheeses, beers, poets or whatever. What's wrong with the word selected or chosen? And why are reading series curated and not simply organised? Where this will all end, I've no idea, but I can envisage some pretentious arse rabbiting on about curating their own bookshelves one of these days. Lord help us.

The Table is just one of the art galleries in Hay. Further up the road is the Lion Street Gallery with its changing exhibitions of painting, ceramics and sculpture from Welsh and border artists chosen by owner and artist, Brent Blair, who left London for Wales in 2011. Around the corner on Brook Street is the Pottery, which stocks practical and decorative ceramics by well-known studio potters, as well as the terrific garden vessels, and delicate porcelain works from a recent working stay in China potted by owner, Simon Hulbert. I've always been a total sucker for ceramics. My house is full of them, both manufactured and handmade, decorative and in daily use, antique and modern. So, it is pretty hard for me to walk past the Pottery and not go in. If I do that though, it is more likely than not that I will leave with yet another beautiful thing and have a week of eating baked beans.

Hay Makers is a co-operative enterprise in St. John's Place that has been showing and selling high quality craftwork for over thirty years. The range of makers includes jewellers, ceramicists, woodworkers, felt makers, stone carvers, and it is an outlet for the Tuareg goods in silver and leather from the artisans of Hay's twin town, Timbuktu. Years ago I bought an indulgent ego piece in Makers – a large stone paperweight carved with a flourishing letter K by Catriona Cartwright. It sits on my desk keeping unruly work-in-progress poems in some semblance of order.

Opened in 2017, The Drawing Room on High Town is a small and perfectly formed artist run gallery and well worth a good long look. Its mission is to be edgy and unapologetically so. I rather like that and concur that art should function to stir things up, even if it's only open by appointment. But it didn't last and like so many of the little businesses in Hay, it handed over the premises to photography gallery, Thru the Lens, in November 2019. Bluestone Gallery and the Hawthorn Gallery are even newer additions, which both sell the kind of art that matches the sofa (we all have different taste) and more earrings that there are days and earlobes to wear them.

Eirian Studio Glass is just that on Oxford Road. Paul Brown and Rowena Lloyd have been making hand blown glass in their studio/gallery for thirty years. Like ceramics, I have a love of glass, but I've yet to save up for one of their gorgeous pieces, as I am too much of a spendthrift. But one day. Perhaps I'll start dropping some none too subtle hints about my sixtieth birthday.

So that's how many galleries? They might come and go, like the much-missed Bowie Gallery (nothing to do with David), but for a town of Hay's size it's astonishing that there are so many. Their success is no doubt a function of bookish attractions, but in concentration, they also make Hay a destination for the discerning art lover. And it is a joy that art businesses are able to thrive in our straightened times, when art tends to come a very, very distant last.

A FEW BOOKSHOPS MORE

Up Lion Street a few steps from Booth's and I'm outside Addyman's, one of their three bookshops and this one has been here for over thirty years. As well as the main shop ranged over several floors of this building, there's the Annexe on Castle Street, which is where you go for sex, drugs and rock and roll (and philosophy and poetry and, and), and the intriguing Murder and Mayhem just across the road. This latter does what it says on the

tin as for the last twenty years it has specialised in crime of all kinds, Conan Doyle to Agatha Christie to Scandi-noir. If you simply can't live without a comic mug with the legend M is for Merthyr, this is the place for you, perhaps, but not me as I am a snob and I don't do genre. What I admire though is the shop's paintwork, which is green and sleuthy, a suitably kind of palette befitting Sherlock Holmes with hounds pacing below its windows.

Addyman's carries everything from Antiques to Travel. Its interior is weird and wonderful; the staircase, steam punk room,

bat cave, and the interior of a nineteenth century Transylvanian church are worth a visit. Clearly the price of admission must be to buy a book, 'anytime', as the graffito on the side wall outside the Annexe reminds. One must strive at all times to be a good customer as Addyman's strap line is that the customer is always wrong.

Turning onto Castle Street I'm in dangerous territory for an old geographer. Mostly Maps sells heroin in the form of antique maps of the British Isles and beyond. I have also spent many hours trawling its topographical prints. Thankfully these days, I lack the wall space, but that doesn't stop me salivating over the odd vintage OS map, or one of Northern Canada where the coastline fades into white space of the unknown, or an atlas where the Far East is so out of scale as to dwarf Australia. Fascinating.

Ten years ago I would have carried on up Castle Street to the substantial stone built Georgian house that sits on the junction with the Oxford Road, opposite the Blue Boar pub. *À l'epoque*, it was the gardens and gardening bookshop, it's front rooms packed with all kinds of horticultural treasures from Tradescant to Chatto. And the front garden was a showcase for its owners to display their expertise. But the book trade is a fickle one and shops come and go; mainly though they go. Even during the course of writing this book some old stalwarts of Hay have closed their doors for the last time. The King of Hay is no more, nor is Rose's

Books, which lovingly sold children's and illustrated books on Belmont Road, Oxford House Books moved to Spain, and even Boz Books is closed for what seems to be refurbishment. Its space was reconfigured into an art gallery – Ty Tan Arts[41] – by artists Jeremy Stiff and Menna Angharad to show case their paintings and sculpture. Exciting times in Hay when another gallery opens and their work is large scale and fascinating. If only I had room to house it in my tiny London abode.

Other shops close too, such is the present trend on every high street in the country, but in a small market town it seems more obvious and acute. Not that there is a daily need for Welsh goods: dragons, rugby shirts and flags, but it was sad to see the shop that sold them, close its doors in 2017, having been unsuccessfully for sale for four years.

OLD OR NEW?

There are people who will debate for many hours the merits and morals of selling second hand books. Their objections being that the only people who make any money in this enterprise are the booksellers. The authors receive nothing. In these days when non-block buster authors' incomes are so low as to be impossible to live on – surprisingly this is true for novelists and even more so for poets – this might sound like a welcome conversation. Personally, I'd just be happy if a sufficient number of people bought my work, so that the publisher felt able to chance their arm with my next book. I am not trying to make a living at the poetry game, no-one does, everyone has to do something else for money, and so increasingly do literary novelists and others. In my case it was a thirty-five year stretch in corporate consultancy – long hours and a horribly mind and energy sapping commute. If I'd tried to live on my puny royalties, I'd have starved in a garret long ago. But does this entitle me to ask for royalties on second hand book sales?

I think not. Booksellers take the financial risk of buying huge numbers of potentially unsaleable books, which have to be stored in the right conditions. Books are a quasi-consumable in that sense, one leaky roof and the whole lot goes mouldy. And they hardly make much themselves, just look at the number of bookshops in Hay that have closed over the last twenty years. And they have to compete with charity shops, which acquire their stock for free from donations. Adding the administrative nightmare of tracking authors to pay them a royalty, let alone the cost, would put paid to the secondhand book trade once and for all. What a waste of resources that would be. There are, thankfully, not enough M6 toll motorways being built to accommodate millions of unwanted pulped books in their hard core[42].

An analogy might be this – you buy a car brand new, lucky you, and the manufacturer makes a profit from its production and the ownership of its trade names, marks and other elements of intellectual property like its design – one of the things that made you buy that car over another. You drive the car for a number of years until it's clocked up too many miles, so you decide to sell it before it loses too much value. Do you have to pay the trademark owner a percentage? No, you do not. It made its share on the first sale. Books are no different in my view. Pity, but there we have it. This is the business end of writing and nothing to do with literary merit. And if it were otherwise, Hay would be an insignificant and economically depressed market town frequented by its locals, and a few visiting walkers, fishers and canoers. There'd be no thriving arts scene, no festivals, fewer pubs and restaurants and the castle would have been derelict for even more decades. And it would be so much less rich for all that.

READER, I FOUND HER

I don't read too many novels; my days of commuting and devouring a novel a week to block out and lessen the interminal (sic) stress of nearly four hours a day on trains and tubes are, thankfully long over. There is too much poetry and non-fiction for me to read in several lifetimes, so I select my novels with care and limit myself to about a dozen a year, if that. But there is one novel I read and re-read annually, because, well, I love it. Charlotte Brontë's masterpiece, *Jane Eyre*, is the one. Don't ask me to explain why, other than that Jane is the heroine to end all – forthright, moral and kind, she suffers, yet overcomes much before her happy ending with her no longer so handsome prince. And I admire Brontë so much that I named by eldest daughter Charlotte in her honour.

I seem to have acquired several copies of the novel over the years without really trying. My favourite is a leather and marble paper bound edition from 1887, some forty years after it was published under her male pseudonym, Currer Bell. It's not in the greatest condition, scuffed and loved as it has been over the last hundred and thirty odd years; some of its pages are lightly foxed, some towards the end have been ripped and repaired with very old tape, and its end papers were renewed a long time ago. I bought it in one or other of Richard Booth's bookshops long since. It cost a princely, then, three pounds. It has some lovely engraved illustrations, uncut edges and the kind of close typeface that is beginning to test my eyes, but its heft in my hands as I leaf its pages is perfect. Just give me an armchair and a pot of tea.

To test how popular the novel still is in terms of its availability in Hay's bookshops I played a little game the other day; the results of which I share now. How many copies are to be found and how much are you going to have to part with to acquire one?

I started in Hay Cinema Bookshop for no other reason that I was on Castle Street. I found The Brontës' sticker easily enough on the shelf in the right hand side upstairs literature section, but nothing else. Not one volume by any of the sisters. Not even in the Folio Society section. A surprising blank. Addyman's Annexe has some paperback Brontës, but not *Jane Eyre*. She was proving elusive. It's almost as if she'd run away from Thornfield Hall and out across the Yorkshire moors in a rainstorm. On to Hay on Wye

Booksellers, but again, nothing; not a paperback, Folio or nice binding to be seen. Curious. Green Ink Books ditto. Not a copy. Clock Tower Books has a couple of paperbacks: *Shirley* and *Villette*, but no *Jane*. Where was she to be found?

In Richard Booth's bookshop I duly located her in the form of a new Everyman edition for tenner, and in a set along with five other novels by Charlotte and her sisters with nicely gold tooled, but not leather bindings, for the astonishing amount of two hundred quid. What? I must be missing something in my appreciation of antiquarian books, but boy, that sounds like a lot to me, even though I was not looking to acquire another copy *per se*.

Last stop then and last hope was Addyman's proper. Very kindly they let me take my dog into the shop as I am able to carry him. Normally, and quiet understandably, this is verboten. There have been just too many accidents on expensive piles of books for dogs to be lead around the book stacks. But finally it was here that I hit the motherlode of Jane. Juggling dog and bag, downstairs I found the nice Collins edition that I already own for nine pounds – gosh, I must re-evaluate my books. Upstairs I find her in a large 1947 compendium with *Wuthering Heights* and *The Tenant of Wildfell Hall* for a fiver. Who said there are no bargains in Hay? And more, there were two brand spanking new editions to choose from: a nice Chiltern one with a pretty cover for twenty pounds (if you must), and another for £6.95. Thus Jane can certainly be found in fine form in town and for all pockets however deep. This is not a surprise I suppose, she's a perennial, even though I was getting rather concerned about her survival until I reached Addyman's.

Here's a challenge then, dear readers: pick your favourite book and start your own search. Who's got it and what's it going to cost you? No need to tell me, just enjoy a few hours in Hay with a purpose and you might just alight on other things you want to acquire while you are at it. And no cheating by going on-line to seen which shop it stocking what. This is a form of exercise for the otherwise sedentary bibliophile. Up and down those stairs, and in and out of those stacks. Have fun! It might be a game with which to keep fractious children occupied as well. You're welcome.

WHERE THE BLACK LION SIPS

Not a pub review, we've not going there remember, so this is another well in this town of water. It's a roasting summer's day and I'm looking for a quiet place to rest. Easily missed, the turn off at the top end of Lion Street before the Drill Hall, where the Hay Festival has its offices, leads down to the well and to where a stream trills over stones. There's a flit of butterflies and small birds into the willows. Above, jackdaws circle the castle from their roost in its trees and chimneys. They form a huge flock, cawing over the town. For a moment my vision is black with birds. The air is still. And then a breeze. I am sorely tempted to dip my toe into Dulas Brook. Were I to do so, I could be in two countries at once as the border runs right down its middle. Right foot or left in Wales? What would that signify?

Before the dip is the large site of the former car repairer; what town planners call light industrial use. The business moved to Forest Road years ago. All is derelict; a sad corrugated roof and peeling blue paint. Weeds grow up through the concrete forecourt. Piles of rubble are ready to be cleared. It is an uncommon sight in Hay and I can't help thinking it represents an opportunity for someone or something, which proved to be the case as an interesting timber clad house is presently being built there. Hard by is an ancient timber-framed cottage being re-shingled; its skeleton is open to the air like a rib cage during heart surgery. New lead flashing and a redressed chimney make it fit for this century. In micro-focus, these two buildings are the present story of Hay.

Black Lion Green is down here in a little dingle of cottages. It is a welcoming green space and there's the well. Local custom has it that whichever partner to a marriage is first to drink from the well's waters will be the one who 'wears the trousers'. Charming though this is, Black Lion Green was once the site of something much more violent: a stoning by an apparently angry mob of Hay folk, which lead to the victim's death from his injuries. In 1740, more than thirty years before Wesley's visit to the town, an evangelical Methodist, close associate and friend of the Wesleys called William Seward was attacked. His offence? Preaching against enjoying oneself. Railing at local customs, feasting, fairs and general merrymaking was common practice for Methodists. It certainly was in my family well into the twentieth century: my paternal grandmother – three times to chapel on Sundays – referred to card-playing on any day of the week as the devil's cards. Not that it stopped my grandfather from teaching my sister and I to be pretty handy pontoon players, mind.

An anonymous contemporary account has it that "the town at the time was noted for wickedness, and the great spiritual darkness of the people"[43]. It's easy to see why such homiletics didn't go down too well with hard working people deserving of some fun. But Steward was in a league of his own on this, apparently even Wesley considered his views inflammatory. So, it is unsurprising that, as his plaque in Cusop church describes, he was "injured… after he had spoken to the hostile crowds of Hay". I like to think it was a protest that quickly got out of hand, but who knows what the "cowardly ruffian, standing behind the preacher, [who] threw at him a huge stone, which striking his head, caused him to fall senseless to the ground" was thinking. Whatever it was, Seward unwittingly became the first Methodist martyr.

Seward shouldn't have been too shocked by this reception at Hay, although clearly he wouldn't have expected it to be mortal, as on many previous occasions during his preaching tours of Wales earlier that year, he had been met with similar hostility. He was pelted in Newport, almost pulled down from the table he and his companion, Howell Harris, were preaching from and was subjected to much verbal abuse[44]. The mob in Caerleon threw rotten eggs, dung and a dead cat. Seward needed medical attention to an eye wound as a result. Stones, earth, walnuts, a cat and a dead dog greeted him in Monmouth, where Seward received further facial injuries. Fortitude and bravery were the lot of the Methodists on these early missions in Wales. During the week Seward was laid up and dying in the Black Lion Inn, he lived his religion to the end, praying for his attacker and asking that he not be punished. Quite a man. And a man of some substance.

Before his conversion to Methodism on meeting Charles Wesley in 1738, Seward, whose home was at Barsey, near Evesham, worked in London in the South Sea department of the Treasury. His role involved managing the National Debt. This was the remit of the notorious South Sea Company after its famous bubble had burst in 1720 and its subsequent ventures like Arctic whaling, and otherwise exploiting its exclusive licence to trade with the Spanish Indies, failed for a whole variety of reasons, including war, and its profitable slave trading ventures ended in abolition. As a successful businessman, Seward amassed a further fortune (he was from a wealthy family to start with) from his investments, but he was also generous: involved in supporting as many as twenty charity schools in London, and endowing his parish church with an altar table, clock and box pews. He also raised funds for and donated heavily himself to the mission of his friend George Whitworth to America, even buying a ship called the *Savannah* and accompanying him along the eastern seaboard in 1739 to establish an orphanage near the town of the same name in Georgia.

Apparently, memorialised after his death in Charles Wesley's hymn 'A Prayer for the First Martyr', Seward, as God's champion was promised the starry crown of heaven. If this hymn was written with him in mind, it seems fitting.

HIGH TOWN – BRAVE AND NEW

Mad or brilliant, or both. When someone is brave enough to open a new bookshop in Hay, all I can say is chapeau, and again chapeau. Thus the determination of the Boyd Greens, who previously traded exclusively online, to add to the book town with its first new second hand bookshop in four years is a triumph in their well-chosen mix of history, literature and philosophy. Green Ink Books on High Town, right by the Butter Market, which opened in October 2018, is most firmly on my hunting ground list, as it makes for a pleasant change sometimes to get away from old book smell into the freshness of a newly fitted shop. And I love the paintwork. What is that greeny-turquoisey colour called? I wish them all the best of luck in sustaining the business, as everyone does these days with significant on-line selling, and apparently where they started. I hope they will be here for many years to come.

Not only a bookseller, but another new book related venture is The Story of Books[45]. Started by Emma and Oliver Balch and in its small premises on Castle Street, it describes itself as a working museum creating books and telling stories. Thus the kinds of things this social enterprise does include exhibitions, and running workshops on various aspects of bookmaking, and it's not just for kids. And there's more – Balch & Balch is the newly opened

private press bookshop selling books printed by letterpress printers. Their books are very handsome indeed. Another one of a kind for Hay. But yet, in the ever-changing story, the shop closed in March 2020 and in its place is a fascinating art house called The Flaming Lady of Hay, after Matilda de Braose, opened selling strange works, including some scary papier-maché masks for use perhaps beyond mere wall decoration, and the kind of arty clothes I wish I could afford.

MEMORIAL SQUARE – COME BUY, COME BUY

Making my way up The Pavement and onto Castle Street I stop at the corner where angelic-voiced schoolgirls sing a cappella in summer for additions to their pocket money. The castle ahead of me is half-ruined, gothic, and circled by seagulls, crows and jackdaws, which make for an annoying midmorning chorus. It's Thursday and my attention is drawn for the moment by two things: the wall mounted statue of Henry VII high up on the western face of the Cheese Market, and the market itself, bustling away in and around Memorial Square. The statue is carved from white limestone and was erected in 1995. It was made by London sculptor, Edward Folkard (1911-2005), fellow of the Royal

Society of British Sculptors, who regularly exhibited at the Royal Academy, and was commissioned by Steve Feldgate of Hay Retreats.

Clutching the sceptre in his right hand and holding it tightly to his chest and cupping the orb in his left, Henry looks out over the central square of Hay and up towards the castle, his shoulder length hair flowing behind him. Nothing too unremarkable then in the trappings of monarchy and posing a king actively, but what on earth is he wearing? A full-length robe with something a little fru-fru at the collar. It looks like he just got out of bed, although clearly having time to put on his crown and pick up his 'I'm a king' things. Why is he made to look like Hamlet's father in a nightie? and more's to the point, why is he in Hay? Sometimes one can't know everything, but still one can take a moment of pride in a memorial to the first Welsh king of the English as the added plaque reminds. That it is in Hay, a stone's throw from the border, seems entirely appropriate. A sort of subtle bird flip, if you will.

The Cheese Market was (re) built of lovely stone in 1835 by Sir Joseph Bailey (the then owner of Hay Castle) on the site of a much earlier Guildhall. Its upper floor was the Manorial Court receiving fines from tenants and market traders alike. There's a fascinating list of the nineteenth century tolls market traders had to pay on the wall in William Beales, the solicitors office on Broad Street. It

covers every kind of livestock that might be conceivably change hands at the market. Used sometimes as an entertainment space, over its life the Cheese Market was also the town council chambers and hosted various religious meetings, both Non-Conformist and Catholic, and was the Masonic Hall. In 2008 with the help of Heritage Lottery funding, the Hay Community Interest Company (CIC)[46] took it on as a project to preserve the building, and make it earn its keep. Under the rules of the CIC, it can never be sold and its upper floors are available as a beautifully appointed holiday let, even earning small amounts of surplus funds. These form part of the Hay Fund that is available for community interest projects in Hay, both social and environmental. Such things as sponsorship of vintage fairs and the food festival, as well as the research costs of the Hay History Group are within the fund's gift.

The Cheese Market's open lower floor, the Market Hall, forms part of the weekly, 700 year old Hay market and is usually home to sellers of yummy pastries of all kinds, organic vegetables, tribal carpets, cushions and baskets, and a pop up café serving some of the best coffee in town. It looks out onto the square where other traders set up stalls and are selling produce of all kinds from socks, to flowers, to bric a brac, on what is on other days a small car park. Even the fish van comes to the market.

This timing may not have much helped the local Catholics in the days before refrigeration. My mother is fond of relating a tale of her observant grandfather, who made a habit of coming for lunch on Fridays, creating something of a problem for her mother. The fish van came to their village on Tuesdays and Nana didn't have a fridge. Her ingenious, if irreligious solution, to the dilemma of what to serve was to chop up plain boiled chicken as small as possible and make the strongest parsley sauce known to man. She seems to have got away with it for years, or perhaps great grandpa was just too polite to pass comment.

Depending on the time of year and day of the week in Hay, there may be speciality markets of antiques or vintage items, or, as in the last weekend in November, food, complete with a carol singing male voice choir, as it is this weekend that the Christmas lights are switched on. A tingle goes down my spine at various points as I listen to the hearty songs of the Welsh canon from men so bundled up against the cold in their green coats that they look like patriotic duvets. Producers from all around come to Hay to showcase their food wares and you can buy everything from tempting handmade chocolates flavoured with Halen Môn to locally produced cheese to organic vegetables to wonderful bread, and get thoroughly sozzled on Orgasmic cider and locally distilled gin. The vintage fair and flea market, same weekend, next day, spreads out into castle courtyard, which is the place to go if you need a used Barbour or second hand Harris Tweed jacket. Who cannot live without a plaster Jesus or a mud trampled kilim? I can resist the temptations of an eighty-year-old Ukranian shirt, despite its soft linen and intricate embroidery, but the Welsh Italian pizza has my name all over it.

Yet the dangers of spending too much money on things I simply don't need is as nothing compared to those perceived by our forebears, as Kilvert reports: "But when people are going to market on Thursday mornings they would exhort one another to come back in good time lest they should be lead away by the Goblin Lantern, and boys would wear their hats the wrong way round lest they should be enticed into fairy rings and made to dance."[47] Boys being made to dance by fairies doesn't sound too awful against to the threat posed to girls by the fruit-selling goblin men of Christina Rosetti's[48] 1859 poem, Goblin Market, where Lizzie admonishes her sister Laura for answering the goblins' calls (perhaps the equivalent of being lead away by the goblin lantern) to "Come buy, come buy" with these lines:

> Dear, you should not stay so late
> Twilight is not good for maidens;
> Should not loiter in the glen
> In the haunts of goblin men.

Of course, this all comes too late for Laura who already has sucked dry their fruity offerings. She starts to fade away and can only be saved by her sister facing attempted rape by the goblin men to secure the fruit that will sate and cure her hunger. It is curious to me though, this conjunction in folk belief of outside traders, fruit and the unspecified threat to one's personal safety, sexual or otherwise. Again the inexplicable.

Next to the Cheese Market on High Town is the Butter Market. A one storey example of Welsh Greek revival, unkindly described as "an uncouth Doric temple"[49], it was built in 1833 and restored in 1984. Despite its spiky ironwork fence that makes it look like the town lock up, it too is part of the market, as it has always been. More baked goods, craft items, clothes, home wares, vegetables and plants are on offer under its shelter. Even when bricked up during the war, it was associated with food, being used as a storehouse and egg station.

NATIONAL DISH

Or one of them, at least. I'm forbidden from sharing our family recipe for Welsh cakes and its secret ingredient, so don't ask. This is one point on which I agree to do my mother's bidding. It's a squally winter's day, the kind of day when even putting your nose out of doors risks instant frostbite. Still, you need to eat, and some serious comfort food is in order. Nothing better then, than a slowly cooked Welsh classic, cawl, although best left until tomorrow when the flavours will have mingled and it will still be freezing out.

Historically a gutsy peasant stew, or broth depending on how thick or thin you go with the cooking juices and made with cheap cuts like lamb neck, you can upscale it with better pieces of lamb to make it so much more than an everyday dish. Bundle up then and off you go to Smallfarms on Broad Street or Gibbons on Castle Street to buy some best Welsh lamb, straight off the hill. You know where this has come from and it's been nowhere near a freezer. Lamb mind, not beef or ham hock. Both butchers are purveyors of great and local meat and are to be celebrated; there are few towns that can support one independent butcher these days, and Hay is lucky enough to have two. Pick up your necessary vegetables at Castle Greengrocers, and you are all set.

The ingredients for cawl are as varied and you want to make them. Here's my preferred recipe, but as always, experiment away with whatever is seasonal or available and takes your fancy. There's only one rule – you get what you pay for, so buy the very best ingredients you can afford and that preferably don't come chilled and wrapped in plastic. Here's enough to feed four to six hungry people:

> 2lb Welsh lamb, cut into cubes
> One large onion, chopped finely
> One small swede, chopped into bite sized pieces
> Two parsnips, ditto
> Three carrots, ditto disc-wise
> Six potatoes, cubed small so they disintegrate,
> thickening the stew
> Two leeks, sliced disc-wise
> Fresh (or dried) herbs of choice – I usually go for three or four bay
> leaves, a tiny amount of sage chopped up, or some thyme, and a

large sprig of rosemary
Good quality vegetable stock, enough to cover all the ingredients
Olive oil for frying (or your oil of choice)
Salt and pepper
Seasoned flour

I start with a heavy base iron and enamel casserole pot, the one from Ikea that was so much cheaper than those fancy French ones I foolishly left behind for my ex-husband. If you don't have one of these then a ceramic casserole dish will be just fine; you will just need to do the initial browning in a sauce or frying pan.

Fry the onions until golden brown. Roll the lamb in seasoned flour then add to the pan to seal it quickly. You are not trying to cook it. Remove from the pot. Add all the chopped vegetables, except the leeks, stirring well and often to give them a little initial browning. This is for flavour in the finished stew. Put back the onions and meat and stir the whole lot thoroughly. Add herbs and stock. Season well with best Halen Môn and pepper. Stir.

Put the casserole dish in the oven on about 150 or so or less or gas mark 5 or so or less. It should be left to cook for two to three hours. Check it every half an hour or so, or when you remember, and give it a stir. That won't be difficult as the house will be full of delicious aroma. Add the leeks in the last hour.

Serve (preferably the next day) with something green like kale or spinach. If you want to be even more authentic according to some, serve with a slice of good Caerphilly. I like a nice Gorwydd, even if these days it's not even made in Wales, the producer having moved to England. Yum. You're welcome.

DE PROFUNDIS

The names of the lost men are carefully recorded, like the Hay archers at Agincourt before them, there is a list of those too and a memorial bench, which attracts the attention of passers-by at the end of Castle Street, near the Swan Hotel. I'm rather fond of that bench, the like of which, as my mother is wont to say, lends a certain classiness to the town. The war memorial on Castle Square and the Memorial Chapel in St Mary's lists all the names of the fallen of the twentieth century's wars. Twenty-nine and twenty-eight respectively[50] men from Hay and the nearby village of

Cusop were killed. Some share surnames; brothers or cousins, I imagine. And then I multiply this number across the Wales, every town and village, across the rest of the UK, across France, across the rest of Europe, across the Commonwealth (or Empire as it was).

The scale of these wars is hard to figure. Incredible. And the grief, I cannot begin to even imagine. That is why I have had a little bit of a problem with too much jollity in the recent centenary of the 1914-18 conflict. There's been rather too much "Oh What a Lovely War" about the place in the last few years for my taste. I'm all for respect, don't get me wrong, but dressing up and playing soldier rather cloys my throat. A hundred years is still too soon for re-enactment. Those who died are with us in living memory. They will only be gone when their names are forgotten. The memorial bench added in the square in 2018, with its silhouetted soldiers and bright red poppies, is a well-designed and subtly appropriate addition to my mind.

My own family, like every other, has its story to tell: the usual wind takes the heat out of a sunny day on the first weekend in August 2015. Northern France. The wheat harvest is in full swing – combines and grain carriers churn across the land with all the efficiency mechanized agriculture can afford. In the sea of golden grain, patient maize and two-tone cattle lie different plots. At regular intervals British and other cars stop beside the fields of white and green that dot the Somme landscape every quarter of a mile or so. The curious, the buffs, the just-passing, the serious historians, the searchers of family history, whatever their motives the passengers spare the time to stand in the corners of these forever England places. Of course, they are more than forever England as the Welsh, Irish, Scots, Australians, New Zealanders, Canadians, Indians, French, and Germans will attest. We came to the Le Tournet Monument in search of one particular grave. And that's a thing in itself. Not all the men slaughtered in this place a hundred years ago were afforded such. The names on the monument, just 13,400 of them here, are all that there is to mark these men. My relative on the other hand has a headstone, a beautiful piece of creamy marble, kept moss and lichen free by the commendable Commonwealth War Graves Commission. On it, under the Prince of Wales feathers of the Welsh Regiment and above the simple cross are his name, J. Lewis, his rank – Private – his army number and the date he died, 13 February 1916.

What is missing is that he was John Lewis, my great, great uncle, and that he was only twenty when he was the target of a German sniper early on a Sunday morning in the bitterest month of winter. I remember my great-grandmother telling me about her lovely brother when I was a small girl. We have photographs of him. We have a geology book he inscribed. Here we are then, nearly one hundred years later, taking a pause in our busy lives, feeling rather goose bumpy, writing a message in the visitors' book, taking pictures, and making a mental note of where he is. If you stand one metre to the left of the right hand pillar at the entrance to the monument and look towards the oak tree, his grave is directly in front of you in the fourth row in front of the tree, beside four other Welsh boys, all about the same age, all killed just days apart.

And even if they did come back from the war, it was not necessarily to their homes. As Gill[51] points out in his autobiography when writing about the post First World War ruined countryside near Hay at Capel-y-Ffin: "The population of the [Llanthony] valley was but a quarter of what it had been fifty years before... The young men had gone to the mines and were wandering unemployed in the Rhondda. Their fathers could not call them home for the city of London found it more profitable to foster Australian Capitalist sheep farming than to preserve the thousand year traditions of the South Wales mountains." One might be writing a similar *crie de coeur* any day now as Brexit takes its toll on our agricultural economy.

ST JOHN'S PLACE – WESLEY WORDS

Now mainly a rather swanky eatery, the higgledy-piggledy stone buildings of St John's Place, on their own island in the centre of town, have a fascinating and vivid history. To see the Jacobean wall-mounted carvings for yourself you'll have to peek through the door when the chapel is open. Here is a site that started life as a mediaeval guild chapel, founded in 1254.[52] This meant it was the place of worship for the tradesfolk of Hay, especially early on market days, as well as serving as the castle garrison's chapel. A merchant guild, as this was, is to be distinguished from the more familiar craft guild. It was an association to monopolise trade in a town, which set and monitored trading standards and the quality of goods, typically food, cloth and other staples, and sought to control prices. These guilds were also, as we might say, a lobby group to the lord of the manor, advocating for the economy of the town that its members controlled. Non-guild members wanting to operate in Hay at this time would have had to pay fees for the privilege to these most influential people.

Quite why any of this proto-capitalist commercial activity needed a place of worship, I don't understand. I need to be reminded that religion was central to public life in a way that is simply isn't today. Church attendance, although not actually compulsory for another three hundred years, was a commonplace expectation. Thus members of a guild were also members of the church dedicated to St. John, paying fees to provide for a priest, and operating something of a social service, as such chapels also set up hospitals and, as here in Hay, a school, as well as being a social safety net assisting the poor.

Thus St John's chapel operated centrally to Hay's life for just over three centuries until its dissolution in 1547. Edward VI, under the guidance of Archbishop Cranmer, continued the countrywide Reformation work of his father, Henry VIII, and the seizure of further church lands and properties. The site was then given to the Vaughan family in 1567. Roger Vaughan, from a long line of Clyro Vaughans, was at various times sheriff of Radnorshire and Brecknockshire, commissioner of the peace in Radnorshire, Herefordshire and Brecknock, and MP for Radnorshire.

Fast forward another couple of hundred years and the chapel is noted as being a ruin in 1774 when John Wesley preached there. Hay was just one stop during a lifetime of travelling the country by the founder of Methodism. He rode something like a quarter of a million miles, preached over 40,000 sermons, and published over 400 texts; a hugely impressive output that makes me look like a slouch. In 1811 the chapel became the town lock-up for the next sixty odd years, presumably once the part of the castle that had been used as such was abandoned. Its first occupants in this incarnation as a drunk tank were the labourers building the horse drawn railway. Over time, a fire station, school, and shops (butchers, saddler's, barber, bank), and later a house, on Thursdays at 10am, there is still a Mass.

A NEW CHAPTER

Or to be precise, Chapters[53]. Located in St John's Place this is the newest of Hay's eateries (as of writing in 2019), and is run by a young and very capable team of first time restauranteurs Charmaine Blatchford and Mark McHugo. It is certainly a place worth dining. I know, I said this wasn't a book with such a guide, but in this case, I am prepared to make a major exception. The trouble with booking a table for one is that you often end up being seated at the worst one in the house, namely, with a view of the kitchen, and Chapters is not the open kitchen kind of place that were popular in past years. However, I am forgiving and, as I was interested in the goings on behind the scenes, this actually suited my purpose rather well. What I didn't like, though, was the restaurant entrance, which inexplicably avoids the beautiful gothic wooden door, surely the space's best feature, and leads you around the back past both the kitchen windows and the bathroom. I might rethink that for the sake of the extra table for two.

The décor is cream walls, and a green ceiling, which probably unintentionally makes the place seem smaller than is necessary. Plain wooden tables are unadorned. I'd like white cloths please, but I know they take work in the laundering. Ubiquitous sempervivums that are all the rage just now and bang on trend air-cleaning house plants are the accompanying greenery. They are small, but the good thing about plants is that they will grow and make more of a statement in the future. The walls are adorned with rather small and predictable prints of fruits, vegetables and herbs. I think I'd bin these and use the wall space as an opportunity to show some large and much more interesting art by many of the talented local or local-ish artists living in and around Hay.

Chapters has two services a day at lunch and dinner from Wednesday to Saturday, which is fine, even if dinner starts rather early at 6pm. Using seasonal and local ingredients in modern British cuisine, the kitchen has two set evening menus: the continuingly bookishly named Chapters One and Two. The former is five courses; the latter seven. I opted for Chapter One, as I don't think I've ever managed more food than that ever in my whole life and look, I really don't need to eat two puddings.

Perfectly spiced mixed nuts appeared immediately while I chose my glass of wine. In a restaurant of this class my heart did sink a little when I saw a drinks menu with so much beer and lager on it. There is no need, really. I mean, wine with food, always, and if you desire some hops there are plenty of hostelries in Hay which can supply these any day of the week. I'm a bit of a snob when it comes to wine: French first usually, a result of having lived in Paris for a long time, but here I settled for a glass of Sicilian Pinot Grigio. It was summer and I'd had enough rosé in Provence prior to this dinner. The wine had a nice body and not too much fruit. One addition could be to have more choice of wine by the glass, as there are only two of each colour, for those of us who don't want to neck a whole bottle.

I started with rye bread locally milled down the road at Talgarth. I asked in advance for the gluten free version, as I am intolerant and try to avoid the stuff as much as I can. Gluten free bread is a hit and miss affair and is generally rather dry and scone-like in consistency, so no surprise here that it crumbled under my knife, but I did like the accompanying yeast butter. Think a slight taste of marmite, if you will. Purists will say that quality butter shouldn't be messed around with. I beg to differ.

Next came a little amuse-bouche not on the menu in the form of a chewy sesame and nut caramel cracker topped with two mousses – chorizo and blue cheese. This was a taste of things to come as many of the dishes that followed had blobs of highly flavoured mousse. These were incredible delicious; little hits of intensity on the tongue. I was tickled though as to why the cracker needed to be served on a flat stone. That trend of presenting food in bizarre containers has always made me laugh. Thankfully it was the only example this evening.

The first proper course was a heritage tomato salad – meaning three different varieties at least, with goats cheese two ways – one mousse, one pieces – and a summer herb (mainly basil) velouté, or sauce to you, and which was poured at the table. I like that fine dining approach to presentation. It shows care and attention to the dish, which being thoroughly delicious in every way, was what it deserved. I am biased though, as I absolutely adore tomatoes and could have eaten more.

Following in rather quick succession came soused mackerel with radishes in thin slices and little whole ones, and gooseberry dashi or blobs of sauce. Yum. I learned long ago, I think from Keith Floyd (remember him?), that gooseberries go very well indeed with mackerel. Their sweetness cuts through the oiliness of the fish and stops it from being overpowering. Add the pepperiness of a few small geranium leaves and I pretty much inhaled this exquisite combination.

The lamb three ways came rather too quickly. I'd liked to have had a little pause at this point before being presented with yet another dish. Locally sourced from the Black Mountains, this was the best of Welsh lamb in the form of perfectly pink rump and well-cooked back and a little tartlette of mixed cuts in a tasty sauce. The trouble with lamb in general is that it tends to be fatty in the meat itself, so I prefer every trace of fat to be cut off. Not to worry though as I surreptitiously slipped my dog a tidbit. I do realise that was appalling behaviour on my part, but I think I got away with it. The lamb was accompanied by roasted new potatoes and aubergines with pickled courgettes and 'gravy' again poured at the table. A great variation on the Sunday roast.

And finally, a rest and a chance to look around at my fellow diners. I spot the inevitable couple who have been so long a couple that they have completely run out of things to say to one another. Though in different guises, they are always to be found in restaurants across the land and they never fail to make me smile in a been there done that and no longer kind of way.

To finish there was a dark chocolate delice, which was a kind of slice tart without a base, topped with chewy sesame crackers and blobs of lighter chocolate mousse. This was sided – oh, check that word – by a just tart enough blackcurrant (grandmother's blackcurrants I learn later) ice cream and all set on a blackcurrant coulis. And it was at this point I failed. I knew I would. The chocolate defeated me, and embarrassingly, I had to leave a little of it behind. A great pity as the fruit and chocolate combination was to die for.

Children are welcome at Chapters and are accommodated by tasting menus of the set menu. Dogs are welcomed too with a cheery smile, which is just as well, as I'd rather not have left my little boy in the car. But what is most unwelcome is the choice of music. I am so fed up with rock music and the like from the 1960s and 1970s. I really don't want to listen to The Kinks and The Doors while I'm eating. Honestly. This must be a generational thing; perhaps this sound track is retro and hip to the owners, but to me it is as jaded as hell. You can keep your 'Riders on the Storm' to yourself, and as for expecting me to savour and digest while Paul McCartney and Wings are singing. Pleeease, no!

That said, the whole experience was a delight to my palate. I can't recommend the food here more highly. I wish the owners every success in taking Hay by gastronomical storm for many years to come. If you are planning to come to the festival or anything else here, make sure you book your table at Chapters well in advance as I expect they will be constantly and so deservedly sold out. Five stars for the food, service and welcome. Three for the décor and drinks. £43.50 including the wine. Don't miss it.

MARKET STREET – GAUDY DAYS

Rummaging around the Antique Market on Market Street, I have nothing in particular in mind, just a good browse, or a bit of stocktaking, by which I mean checking the prices of things similar to those that I own. Cheeky, but I'm sure I'm not the only one who does this. I look with horror at the unbelievably cheap prices of the brown furniture. Why doesn't anyone want to own anything Victorian and Edwardian? It is made of the most incredible woods that can never again be harvested. Mahogany, rosewood, tulip wood, ebony, indeed anything from the world's rainforests are going to be so rare. Why can't anyone see this? Why do people prefer chipboard from Scandinavia that you have to assemble yourself? And how can anyone commit the crime of so-called up-cycling? Painting mahogany, or anything else that's been painstakingly French polished, should be outlawed. Unbelievable.

Calming myself down, I am drawn, as always, to a certain type of brightly glazed ceramics. Cobalt blue, burnt orange, yellow, red, green and copper lustre, it's Welsh Gaudy. Some think it indeed gaudy and I confess its brashness is not exactly to my taste; I'm more of an Art Deco girl, but it holds a special place in my heart. Years ago my mother's dresser filled up with the stuff; some of it inherited – it was the china put behind glass, barely used and meant for showing off, some purchased at auction or in her forays into the depths of antique shops the country over, including here at Hay. To say I grew up with it would be about right. Tea cups, saucers, plates, pots and milk jugs shone through my childhood. No surprise that it still brings joy to my eye.

Welsh Gaudy is not posh porcelain.[54] Produced between about 1820 and 1860, it was relatively cheap and meant to be an everyday or cottage ware, although one person's everyday was my great-grandmother's best. She had that right, as there are now significant collections in the museums of Cardiff, Swansea and Merthyr. Over two hundred patterns have been catalogued, all of them containing a large amount of the distinctive cobalt blue in their design: the tulip, the oyster and the smoking Indian seem to be the most popular, but there are also designs called wagon wheels, or containing daffodils, grapes and vines, or named after places from Snowdonia to Capel Curig to Caernarfon. It was manufactured in Wales at Swansea and Llanelli, hence its original name, Swansea Cottage, but the bulk of it was made in Allerton's Staffordshire pottery. Sold in the UK domestic market, as well as being exported to America, it was popular, particularly with Welsh émigrés in places like Pennsylvania, and where its new name arose.

In the history of ceramics, it is considered important as marking the transition from exclusively had produced wares to mass production. Hand painted with varying degrees of skill and flair, a well-executed jug or plate can set you back a pretty penny these days. But only if it's in mint condition, and I'm not entirely sure that the pieces I will inherit one of these days are entirely perfect. No matter.

Other stalls in the market offer every kind of 'antique' you might be in search of. It is an Aladdin's cave of treasures, more and more these days containing newly designated collectables such as mid-century wares, by which is meant ceramics and furniture often of Scandinavian design. If blond wood and troika are your thing – they are not mine – you are well served here. Similarly Welsh wool blankets are, if no longer ten a penny, then at least available. Choice pieces of silver, spectacular china and glass and well, every kind of curio and furnishing, farmhouse or otherwise, clock, picture and vintage costume is here to be discovered from any of the twenty or so dealers' stalls and cabinets of collectables. Eclectic is a word, and the whole is housed in a lovely Georgian building. Take your time. There's no pressure, and you might just find a real gem.

CASTLE STREET – WHERE ALL ROADS LEAD

I look up to the castle, the largest and most imposing building in Hay, and start on its details. The Marches, the collective name for the towns and land either side of the Welsh-English border, had, at least until the sixteenth century, a turbulent history as it took the Norman kings literally hundreds of years from 1066 to conquer Wales. Murray describes the Marches as "a space that was not so much a border or dividing line as a strip of autonomous country where no outside writ seemed to run."[55] The Welsh did not agree to peace in 1536 without some hellish fighting. Hay's story is no exception. Its tale is one of sieges, fires and destruction on the orders of variously King John, Llywelyn the Great, Edward I, and Owain Glyndŵr, as well as legends about the badass owners of Hay castle, inhabiting a border country that "allows…escape [from] the idea of a totalizing allegiance... a cultural outlaw... liberating, stimulating, desirable…"[56] If one looks at the OS map of Hay[57] and its surroundings, one will find lots of features like castle, castle earthworks, moat, motte, motte and bailey, all testament to the notion that every hill in these parts needed a defensive structure of some kind. Hay castle is the best preserved of these local features as it is so much more than indecipherable lumps and bumps in fields or hidden by trees.

Hay was established by one of the Norman Marcher Lords[58], Bernard de Neufmarché, who had defeated the Welsh king, Bleddyn, at the battle of Brecon in 1093. It is thought that he built the motte and bailey, where the livestock market and the main tent of the Hay Winter Weekend are now located, as a reconnaissance post, the main castle being started much later. There's not much more now to that first castle than a small rise in a field. After 1115 Hay really began its development with the dedication of St Mary's church and English and Anglo-Norman tenants were granted burgage tenements. These plots of land were paid for by cash rent rather than feudal service, and something of their layout can still be seen in the long thin back gardens of some houses in Hay.

The Neufmarchés were disinherited of Hay by Henry I on account of the misjudged behaviour of Bernard's son, Mahael. Apparently[59], on discovering his mother was having an affair, he beat up her lover. Nest, was not best pleased and complained to the king citing Mahael's legitimacy. With one eye on maintaining peace with the Welsh as Nest was descended from Prince Gruffydd ap Llywelyn, Henry handed Hay to Mahael's sister Sibyl, who he married off to Miles of Gloucester, the English High Constable, thus keeping Hay in loyal hands at least for a while. Miles was unluckily shot in a hunting accident in the Forest of Dean, so his four sons succeeded to the castle in turn, but since none of them had any children, Hay passed to their sister Bertha and her husband, William de Braose. It is their son William and his wife Maud (also known as Matilda) who are our badasses.

William and Maud de Braose ruled their fiefdom with iron fists. In 1175 William held a supposedly reconciliatory Christmas feast in Abergavenny for Seisyll ap Dyfnwal, the Welsh leader, and his key followers. This turned out to be a blood bath as William suspected Seisyll of murdering his uncle and sought revenge by despatching his guests. Think of movie action in *The Godfather*, or of Al Capone and the baseball bat, if you will. Nice guy.

To expand their lands William and Maud raised an army against the Welsh, which in 1198 was victorious at the Battle of Painscastle. This event earned William his baby-eating monster reputation in local lore. Maud too had mythical status as the giantess who built Hay castle in one night. The truth, of course, is more mundane, the castle started life in the late twelfth century as a motte and bailey, which was sacked by Llywelyn in 1233. Today's stone castle was developed over the succeeding centuries. And Maud was praised by Gerald of Wales as an excellent woman, prudent, chaste and a marvellous housekeeper, which is a flattering portrait of her in contrast to her centuries' old reputation as a demon-conjuring witch.

The de Braoses enjoyed nearly a decade of doing exactly as they pleased before they came under the scrutiny of King John. In 1207 John suspected them of stealing revenue and demanded their sons as hostages to prove their loyalty. Maud refused and publicly accused John of murdering his nephew, Prince Arthur of Brittany. Outraged and enraged, John captured Hay. William fled first to Ireland and then France, where he died at the Abbey St Victor in Paris, which was dissolved during the French Revolution. Its site is the current Jardins des Plantes and Museums. It is odd to think of William's bones under the tamped chalk and chestnut walkways of these genteel gardens. Maud and her eldest son William had the fate of nightmare. Captured by John they were taken to Corfe Castle in Dorset (some say Windsor, but the precise geography is not really relevant to the tale) where they were walled up in a chamber and, of course, starved to death. Shudder. A grim end indeed.

With historical fascinations such as these, it should be no surprise that Matilda became the subject of a historical novel. Barbara Erskine, wrote Lady of Hay in the 1980s, when she lived nearby. It became a bestseller, earning Erskine a Romantic Novelists' Award and a Thumping Good Read Award, and it even had a twenty-fifth anniversary edition. Ingeniously Erskine weaves the tale of a modern day journalist setting out to debunk past-life regression, but ending up reliving Matilda's life during her hypnosis. Erskine says it is as much a biography as a novel and she did a great deal of research for it.[60] It certainly captures the imagination, if you have the stamina for its over eight hundred pages, and not just for its readers, as Erskine is the proud owner of a white glazed pottery figure of Matilda made for her by Adam Dworski, whose Wye Pottery was in Clyro.

William's relatives Giles, Bishop of Hereford, and Reginald fought to maintain the family estates enlisting the help of Llywelyn the Great, but King John fired Hay castle and the town in 1215.

Reginald finally made peace with the English crown, now in the hands of Henry III. But it would seem the de Braoses neglected to make lasting peace with the Welsh as the last William was hanged by Llywelyn the Great in 1230 having been found in his wife's bed chamber.

Thus William's wife, Eva, took charge of Hay, building the town walls for example, and on her death in 1244, the estate was divided between her daughters. Eleanor and husband Humphrey de Bohun inherited Hay, but Eva's sister Maud's husband, Roger Mortimer wanted a fairer distribution. He eventually won Hay as a result of his service at the Battle of Evesham in 1265, but didn't keep it long, as a few year's later, and in receipt of a no doubt generous amount of compensation as part of Edward I's policy of stabilising the Marches, Hay reverted to the de Bohuns. This family became part of English royalty as daughter Eleanor married Thomas de Woodstock, the youngest son of Edward III. Daughter Mary went one better, marrying Henry IV and so was the mother of Henry V.

Marches stability was not easily maintained in succeeding centuries though, as the Welsh under Owain Glyndŵr continued to defy English rule: "that most lewd rebell", according to Englishman and Headmaster of Westminster school, William Camden (1551-1623)[61]. It is important to remember that the lawlessness in the Marches stemmed from the King's writ not applying. As Murray[62] explains: "it was impossible to pursue an offender from England into the March or force an offender from the March to answer for an offence committed in England or against an Englishman. More than this, inside the March a series of lordships ruled, each with its own system of justice run by the individual Marcher lord who had the power of life and death over his people. The March became a kind of launch pad for raids and kidnappings, and merchants who were robbed while in this territory could expect no legal redress."

In 1402 Hay castle prepared for a siege by Glyndŵr that never came and it only suffered minimal damage, which is probably why today the castle ruins still have one of the oldest wooden defensive gates in the country. As you look at the castle from Castle Street, the left hand part of the portcullis gate's oak door dates from some time in the thirteenth century. It is presently causing some issues for the castle restoration project in terms of how to preserve it, yet allow the doorway to be used. A couple of years later in late 1404 the castle was under the command of Sir John Oldcastle, who had the commission to prevent arms and provisions reaching the Welsh rebels.

Oldcastle was born to a knightly family in Herefordshire in 1378, or perhaps as early as 1360, it's not clear. By the time he came to Hay he represented Herefordshire as knight of the shire in Parliament. Later he served as a Justice of the Peace and High Sheriff of the county. An advantageous marriage to Joan, heiress of Cobham, brought him the title Lord Cobham in 1408, along with manors in Kent, Northamptonshire, Norfolk and Wiltshire, and Cooling Castle. As a result of his exemplary military service to Henry IV, including in France and presumably executing his duties in Hay, he became one of the most trusted of the king's soldiers. He was also a great friend and advisor to the Prince of Wales, the future Henry V.

Sound familiar? Well, if you know your Shakespeare, he should do, as he was taken as the model for the roguish knight, Sir John Falstaff, even if the epilogue of *Henry IV Part 2* discredits the likeness. Here, in a protest too much, Shakespeare writes of the future play *Henry V*: "Falstaff shall die in a sweat, unless already a' be killed with your hard opinions; for Oldcastle died martyr, and this is not the man…". However like his future portrait, Oldcastle eventually fell very far from the king's favour. Accused of heresy for his support of the Lollards, Oldcastle was hung and burnt, possibly whilst still alive, in 1413. His tale is one that would not look out of place in any of Shakespeare's plays, involving variously as it does the testing and straining of his relationship with the king; as a leading supporter of Wycliffe and a religion separated from the mediation of the Pope and priests with the Bibles in English, without the pomp and ceremony of the existing Mass and where idolatry was a sin – the fact that eventually did for him; ignoring royal summonses; ex-communication; offering a sworn statement of loyalty to the king that was refused; asking for trial by knights or by single combat, which were also refused; eventual trial; a stay of execution from a king who still considered him a friend; escape from the Tower of London; plotting against the king in a full scale Lollard conspiracy to establish Oldcastle as regent, the abbeys dissolved and the nobility under control; wounding in the insurrection at St. Giles' Fields; another trial;

escape to the Marches, where he hid out for years despite a huge reward on his head; other plots and rebellions against the king; capture and death. A pretty breathless life of action and intrigue in his last four years.

Via Eleanor, Hay passed to the Dukes of Buckingham. Never able to quite pick the right side in the Wars of the Roses and subsequently, they were variously killed at the Battle of Northampton (1460, the first Duke), beheaded for treason (for switching sides to Henry Tudor) in 1483 by Richard III (the second Duke), and executed for treason (a suspected coup) by Henry VIII in 1520 (the third Duke). By the time Henry VIII granted Hay to James Boyle, its strategic military importance had completely diminished.

THE MUCH SOUGHT CASTLE

Until it was stopped during the present large-scale part of the restoration works, the castle tour started on Thursday mornings at 11am. The small group I joined started off through the gateway in the grey stone wall to the right of the war memorial on Castle Street and up the increasingly rickety wooden steps that lead to the scheduled ancient monument and grade one listed castle. Whilst one can wander around the outside, peer in the windows

and enjoy the garden, the only way to gain access to the inside was to take the tour. This is something like democracy in action. Until relatively recently the castle was off limits to nosey parkers like me, having been in private hands, and partly shielded from town by thick shrubberies and mature trees, it was designed to be secluded, even though at some points during the eighteenth and nineteenth centuries the mediaeval cellars were used as the town lock up. But the tour tells me of everything that's been hidden.

First the Norman tower is pointed out and then the door in the portcullis gate. Running out of the wind around the side of the unstable and impassable ruins, one turns away from the terraces that are the remains of the eighteenth century formal gardens into the current gardens. Well, more accurately, its large lawn. Looking at the castle from behind as it were, or the front depending on your perspective, you can see the Tudor part of the house that was built beside and into the Norman tower and which is also ruined due to another fire.

The main part of the currently extant castle is in truth is no more than a large Jacobean house started by James Boyle in about 1660, only added to in the interior and outbuildings overlooking the narrow surrounding lanes. It is a fine stone construction with the kind of twisted brick chimneys that mimic Hampton Court and other palaces.

After the Gwynn family's ownership in the eighteenth century,

the castle was divided into apartments. It was later converted back into a house. A hundred and fifty years ago Kilvert was a frequent visitor to the Bevan family who then occupied it. He writes of tea parties, playing croquet on the extensive south facing lawns and shares his charmingly frank observations about certain young ladies. In the nineteenth century then, it was a wealthy vicar/arch deacon's residence.

In 1914 Country Life came to write a photo-illustrated piece on the castle and its then owner the Lady Dowager Glanusk. The easterly part of the house was destroyed in a fire in 1939 during the ownership of Benjamin Guinness, who from 1935 used the castle as a grand bolt-hole from London and fishing lodge. It has not, as yet, been rebuilt.

Richard Booth bought the castle in 1971 from Edward Tuson of the Studt fairground family who did not live in the castle, but used it as a fancy storage facility for their carousels and equipment. For forty years Booth had a bookshop, Hay Castle Books, in its major ground floor rooms. The place overflowed with books and prints and was hard to manoeuvre around, but allowed for hours of contented browsing in my memory. It smelled of must and damp and book home. As a teenager, I remember finding something to read and hiding myself in a corner to avoid my time-to-go-parents. I wished that one day they would drive off and just leave me there. I know I would have been supremely happy in the book stacks and garden, which Booth used to allow visits to on the payment of 50p, for which to be honest, I'm not sure I ever coughed up.

In 1977 a log rolled out of the fire one of the upstairs rooms and yet again the castle was alight. On this occasion the roof was destroyed. The half-blackened beams and lightning bolt repairs in the currently stripped rooms evidence yet another act of destruction. It seemed this poor building was going to eventually burn itself out.

During the early years of the Hay Festival in the 1980s events were held in the castle, readings and parties were the order of the day. At other times the castle was the setting for uproarious private parties, investitures of princes and nobles, beautifications, and other formal gatherings in its throne room under the auspices and largesse of the self-proclaimed King of Hay. One of Booth's duchesses was April Ashley[63]. In the 1950s, she was one of the earliest people in the UK to have gender reassignment surgery, although she had to travel to Casablanca for it. She came to Hay in the 1970s very much down on her luck and health. Having been outed in the national press in the early 1960s, her modelling and film career was effectively over. She had married an aristocrat in 1963, but that relationship was annulled in 1971 as the court held she was still a man; a ruling that did not change until the Gender Equality Act of 2004 for which she was a prominent lobbyist. She scraped a living as a restaurant hostess in Chelsea until she suffered a heart attack. In Hay her luck changed as Booth lent her a flat and she became carer to an old man who eventually left her a property. When sold, this gave her the funds to move to the US. Super-glamorous Ashley contributed to Hay's flamboyant reputation, and more. She was given an MBE in 2012 for services to transgender equality and in her hometown Liverpool Museum staged an exhibition of her life for eighteen months between 2013 and 2015[64] under the very fitting title, Portrait of a Lady.

Booth sold the castle in 2011 to the Hay Castle Trust[65], a charity with an impressive board of directors including Peter Florence and Elizabeth Haycox, and which now has the task of restoring and regenerating it. The Heritage Lottery fund has chipped in the nearly £4.5 million it is going to cost and the charity has to find £1.5 million. Every £5 tourist like me who took the tour helped. We shall have to watch and wait before the galleries and exhibition space, community rooms for hire, bookshop, wedding venue, restaurant and so on materialize. I for one am looking forward to taking in the fabulous view from the proposed platform on the Norman tower. Perhaps the plans will be modelled on the very successful restoration of Cardigan castle, who knows, but once the infestation of death watch beetle is dealt with, it won't be allowed to fall into any more rack and ruin, or have its fittings spirited away by royalty[66], and will reinvigorate the community and economy.

Hurrah for that, and roll on its opening, whenever that will be, building delays and pandemic permitting. The public is waiting with bated breath, but things are looking good. Internal works are advancing apace and the external entrance-ways are looking stunning. There are two staircases up the castle, one leading to that special door, and another double stair replaces the rickety wooden entrance bridge to the 'house'. Both are built of nicely dressed stone with a huge stone stepped seating area behind the war memorial. It's going to be fabulous.

Jackdaw

I'm the left and right of it
where black and white meet and meld
the proof of complication
ambiguous   a compromise
of this and that that and the other

I shade ruins above tidy town
tussock and castle-tumbled stone
rampart where worms
have worked   composting the midden

I'm the right and left of it
where white and black meld and meet
complication's proof   a compromise
of that and this   the other and that   ambiguous

At wood's edge I'm bleeding light
first rays and long shadows   the start
of chorus and roost   a folded/unfolded wing
out/back from hunting

I'm where black and white meet
the meld of it left and right
proof   complication   a this   that
the other ambiguous compromise

By ring roads I'm straggle trees
leaf-sooted by fungus   where gall hides

home of hoardings sodium glare
drive-by pace to anywhere.

THE GODLY CRUSADES

Explaining religion is a tall order, and for me, a difficult one as I'm more than a bit meh! when it comes to god stuff. I crave your indulgence, if that isn't too profane a request. There's no record of where in Hay the Archbishop of Canterbury, Baldwin, preached a sermon on 7 March 1188, but he was in town that day and night as part of his progress through Wales. We might take a wild guess and have him standing somewhere below the castle in the square addressing the good people of Hay. We know of his presence though, as it was recorded by one of his accompanying canons, the Archdeacon of Brecon, Gerald of Wales, in his *Journey Through Wales*.[67] Of their Crusades recruiting mission to Hay, Gerald notes:

> After the sermon… we saw a great number of men who wanted to take the Cross some running towards the castle… leaving their cloaks behind in the hands of their wives and friends who had tried to hold them back.

This is an unsurprising response of desperate families who knew they were unlikely to see their menfolk ever again if they disappeared to the Holy Land in a fit of valour to defend Christendom.

Prolific writer, Gerald, son of a Marcher Lord, and more Norman than Welsh by blood, had the reputation for being something of a zealot, amongst other things stopping the parish priest of Hay from sharing his benefices with his brother. He was ambitious to the point of being obsessive, turning down four bishoprics having set his sights on St. David's, which he never achieved. He is said, by his own admission, to have been tall and handsome. He had a sharp tongue and a gall-filled way in his writings. I can't help thinking I might rather have liked him for that and for helping us with this brilliant little note in the history of Hay. It certainly enlightens my understanding of the social effect of the Crusades. I don't recall one single history lesson when the human consideration for soldiers and their families was mentioned: loss of family and livelihoods were of no concern over religion and politics in my textbooks. Looking at the present shockingly shoddy state of affairs in UK politics, perhaps I shouldn't be so amazed.

ONE BIG CON

During the eighteenth century Hay castle was divided into apartments for rent. Among the tenants was noted to have been one George Psalmanazar (1679-1763)[68]. Quite what brought him to Hay, when and for how long seems, appropriately, shrouded in mystery, although we might guess that he was in hiding. Conman, hoaxer, and certainly an imposter[69] – indeed, such he was a consummate master of his art that Horace Walpole considered he surpassed the genius of Chatterton, this Frenchman arrived in the UK in 1703. He claimed to be the first native of Formosa (modern day Taiwan) to have visited Europe, having been first kidnapped by Jesuits and taken to France where he refused conversion. Earlier in his life, once he had learnt English, he had tried to travel around France claiming to be an Irish pilgrim on his way to Rome. Too many people were familiar with Ireland, so he was soon rumbled, hence settling on this more outlandish story, but not without first having experimented with being Japanese. Aided by a Scottish priest, Alexander Innes, he was introduced around London.

He is notorious for writing a completely fake memoir – *An Historical and Geographical Description of Formosa, an Island subject to the Emperor of Japan* – with such implausible claims that it is surprising he was able to gull anyone for any length of time at all. Yet the book had two editions and a German translation. I mean, for example, these fabrications included that the men of Formosa wore nothing save gold or silver plates as loin cloths, they dined on serpents, and ate their unfaithful wives, sacrificed thousands of young boys a year to the gods, and lived either underground or on floating islands. Such was the skill of his invention and hyperbole, following his maxim to never amend or contradict himself, that he was even appointed by Oxford University to translate Christian texts into the Formosan language he had entirely made up. He relied on the patronage of and became a favourite of Henry Compton, the Bishop of London and others in London society, such as Sir Hans Sloane and Thomas Herbert, Earl of Pembroke, and he even spoke before the Royal Society. Astonishing, especially if I tell you that he had pale skin and blond hair, any comment on which he dismissed with another lie about Formosan nobles keeping out of the sun. Not surprisingly, eating raw meat and roots was all too much of a pretence to maintain and only succeeded for the period it did because of his literary skills and imagination. The completeness of the world he devised, the facts of which were swallowed whole by a society looking for tales and knowledge of unknown lands like much of Asia, and which had an imperial and missionary vision, had meant that for a while he was in the right place at the right time for financial gain. Psalmanazar also represented a religious success – the conversion of a pagan (by Innes) and a triumph of the English church over the Jesuits.

Coming clean after three years and after being denounced as a fraud by a Walloon minister, Psalmanazar spent the rest of his long life first as an army clerk, until a group of clergymen gave him funds to study theology, and then in London, he worked as a Grub Street hack. Apparently he conducted himself there with a dignified demeanour, even making a friend of Samuel Johnson, who somewhat surprisingly, wished he resembled him. His work was relatively limited to pamphlet writing and editing books. Psalmanazar did however add to his considerable language haul by learning Hebrew. He co-authored, with Samuel Palmer, *A General History of Printing* in 1732. He even contributed to *A Complete System of Geography* of 1747, including writing more accurately about Formosa and engaging in self-criticism of his hoax, which he characterised as youthful vanity.

Not all his literary ambitions succeeded though. His forty pages of a proposed sequel to *Pamela*, Samuel Richardson called ridiculous and improbable. Hardly a surprise there, then. He was satirised by the best – Swift includes him as a proponent of cannibalism in his infamous jest of 1729, *A Modest Proposal,* as "the famous Salamanaazor, a Native of the island of Formosa, who came from thence to London, above twenty Years ago", and Smollett referred to him as "Psalmanazar, who, after having drudged half a century in the literary mill in all the simplicity and abstinence of an Asiatic, subsists on the charity of a few booksellers, just sufficient to keep him from the parish" in his novel *The Expedition of Humphry Clinker* of 1771.

Surviving on a pension from an admirer, Psalmanazar wrote his final memoir in his later years, still keeping secret his real birth name. *Memoirs of* *****, *Commonly Known by the name George Psalmanazar; a reputed Native of Formosa* details his early life and the genesis and development of his imposturing, or so he said. It was meant to be a full renunciation and apology for his fraud and was published after his death. Perhaps, though, we shouldn't forget the small detail of his post-writing daily laudanum taking – "ten to twelve drops in small pint of punch"[70] – not a habit to be dismissed. Never trust a junkie with a goggly-eyed stare and a furrowed brow.

BELL BANK – ONE CHAPEL MORE

Up on Bell Bank is Salem Chapel, the oldest of Hay's Non-Conformist chapels. It was originally built in the 1650s and was rebuilt in 1814 and again in 1878 in a plain-ish gothic style. Today it comprises two buildings: the chapel proper with its yellowing stones and dozen or so graves and memorials in its front yard, and the adjacent and much older unused schoolhouse. The whole is a rather sad looking, bordering on the neglected. Indeed, after a storm that damaged the roof in 2016, it was not all together clear who owned the chapel and was responsible for its upkeep –

not the Baptist Union, but some private trustees who can't seem to be traced. The Hay CIC, which was responsible for the redevelopment of the Cheese Market, stepped in to prevent these important buildings falling into dilapidation and work is in progress to restore them. They are important, not just because they are attractive historic buildings in Hay, but because the chapel was the second Baptist chapel built in Wales by John Myles, and is the oldest extant.

Myles or Miles, the spelling, as so often is the case, is fluid, was born in Ilston on the Gower in 1621. He was educated at Brasenose College, Oxford and became part of the Particular Baptist community in London. Returning to the Gower, he became a minister at Ilston between 1649 and 1662. He was also a tryer of ministers during Parliamentary rule, meaning he was involved in the appointment of church elders and hearing objections to and charges made against them. On the restoration of the monarchy in 1660, all churches were required to use the Anglican Book of Common Prayer. Non-Conformists rejected this prayer book. This was the catalyst for separatist Myles and a wide congregation of around two hundred Baptists to leave Wales in 1663 for America and the Plymouth colony. The Ilston book, now in the collection of Brown University in the US, lists their names, along with the other church records in Welsh. Myles founded the town of Swansea, Massachusetts, and the First Baptist Church in the state there, but only after he and his followers had been asked to leave Rehoboth for their Baptist views. He was pastor in Swansea for some twenty years, and one of the early Welsh immigrants to the New World. And was not, as we shall see later, the only notable person related to Hay to cross the Atlantic.

QUIRKY

Turning into the top end of Bell Bank from the castle drive on Oxford Road, I pause at the window to watch Chris Bradshaw working in the Black Mountains Bindery. He's un-stitching the tatty pages of an important or much treasured book that has been sent to him for rebinding. I hesitate, not wanting to disturb his flow. After a minute or two he looks up, catches my eye and smiles. I take that as my cue to push open the door.

Over the years I have bought several of his handmade beautiful leather bound and marble papered notebooks for myself and my family. On receiving a watercolour book for one birthday, my mother refused to paint in it as it was simply too lovely to use. Not exactly the purpose of my gift, but she had a point. Chris does make the most gorgeous of books, and of course he will cover, repair and rebind almost anything you want to preserve. He'll even put your initials on them in gold. Hay is a good place to be if this is your gentle craft and you also want to sell books on printing, typography and the like. When not playing his guitar and organising the open mic at The Globe, Chris is in his workshop surrounded by papers, curious tools and the smell of glue.

Today I want to treat myself to a new notebook, but he doesn't have any in stock of the right size. That's not the end of the world, so we chat for a little while until I pluck up the courage to ask him a technical bookbinding question, not that I know the right terms. My query is how to get a neat edge on the small books I make for myself. Chris beckons me over to a large and ancient wooden contraption, under which is an enormous pile of offcuts, the product of perhaps years of work. This paper-guano producing machine is a plough. You clamp the pre-bound quires in place and push the blade over the edges to cut them straight and even, a little like planing wood. "Genius", I exclaim and wonder whether it is worth investing in one.

As well as being teacher to a total amateur like myself, Chris is a poetry hero. He edits and publishes a small nicely printed magazine called Quirk three times a year, and always in time for the Festival. His partner in this venture is another poetry hero, Wayland Boulanger. Anyone who keeps faith with putting poets' words into print deserves much praise. I buy a copy of the latest edition – nice cream paper and smooth matt cover – obviously, and will do so every time I see it. It is five pounds well spent as some of the work from local writers and others in its hundred pages pleasantly surprises me, as does the pleasingly chosen black and white artwork.

BELMONT ROAD – LIGHTING A CANDLE

It's a habit I acquired long ago: I can't pass a Catholic church without going in and lighting a candle for my maternal grandfather, not that he was especially religious. I think it was more custom than faith, but these things are handed down in families, like the silk and lace Christening gown that three generations of us have been christened in, and quickly mind, in the Roman way as it's a small size for very new babies, just in case. Can't risk being left in limbo, can we? Not that his faith passed along. My mother explains the demise of attending Mass due to the War – something about the nearest Catholic church being a few villages or at least a bus ride away. Along comes petrol rationing and out goes the bus service, taking Roman Catholicism with it, or something like that.

I slip beyond the beckoning red of the contemporary abstract stained glass and gothic windows into St Joseph's, or rather I would have slipped into the building had its door not been firmly closed. Ah yes, the end of Roman Catholicism again for today.

It's interior, had I been able to see it, is a surprise: simply painted in cream with a blue ceiling and fitted out with blond wood benches. It is nothing in fact that you might expect from the exterior, and a million miles away from the sumptuous gold of your average Italian parish church. And therein lies a tale. The church was not built for the smallish Catholic congregation of Hay. It was originally the Tabernacle of the Calvinist Methodists

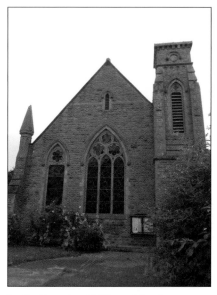

built first in 1829, with the present stone building completed in 1872. It was taken over by the Catholic Church in 1968. I imagine at that point it had a complete make over into its present uncomplicated look.

WARP AND WEFT

Past St Joseph's, and as you walk up hill on Belmont Road, on the left is an imposing grey stone block of flats that takes much looking at for it to reveal its industrial past as Howells' woollen mill. Built in the late eighteenth century, it was the largest one of three woollen mills in Hay owned by Thomas Howells (1749-1819), wool manufacturer, as his gravestone in St Mary's says simply. Here wool was carded, spun, and woven into working shirts for the industrial workers of South Wales. It's not impossible that some of my ancestors wore garments made here. Closed in the mid-nineteenth century when it could not compete with steam-powered woollen mills, at its peak the mill employed up to eighty of the good people of Hay.

Thomas Howells had itchy feet and looked into the possibility of moving to Virginia in 1788. In a cheeky letter he wrote from

Hay to George Washington in 1789[71] he says:

Sir,

I flatter myself you'll readily excuse the Liberty I take in addressing you, when you understand that the following thoughts are the result of a strong attachment to the freedom of America, and a desire of transplanting a manufactory which in time will be found of the greatest consequence—Last year I visited the Continent of America, with a full determination to become a Settler, but finding the Government not in so settled a State as I expected obliged me to abandon the enterprize for the present and wait to see the result of the New Government that was then forming, with a full determination, when permanently fixed, to make an offer of my service to the State of Virginia, to introduce the Woolen Manufactory on the present most approved plans now working in England and in my own manufactory—The great objections made by some that Manufactorys can not at present be introduced with advantage into America, are the Country being thinly settled & labour at present too high—The great improvements which have been made in England in the Woolen and Cotton business by Water-Engines is an amazing saving in labour as much as three fourths through the whole process & in some departments as much as nine tenths.

But supposing the number of young white people, that will be requisite for a large Manufactory can not be easily obtain'd I would propose that those Gentlemen who are disposed to emancipate their Negroes would appoint some of their younger ones for that business and give them their freedom after a service of seven years as an Apprentice, then there will be little doubt but they will remain in the business and become useful Members of Society—this I only propose Sr if there should be a scarcity of hands—but from the population I observed when in America, there will be little to be fear'd from that—As this is a business that will require a large Capital to proceed on a scale that would be likely to turn out to profit, I shall propose to sink of my own real property one thousand pounds in the Trade and with me shall import Engines for cording & machines for slubing and spinning with every other apparatus necessary for the business, with a sufficient number of my best Workmen to take under their care those young people who might be willing to be instructed in the several departments of the business.

From the State I shall expect as a reward for so great a Risk and to make good the Losses that will arise while the Manufactory is in its infant State, a certain Stipend for a given time and a right to a certain quantity of Land a part of which I shall give to my Men as an Encouragement for them to embark in the Undertaking, under certain restrictions that they shall remain in the Manufactory at least 7 years—A House & building necessary for the work must be found—&c. &c.

These Sir are the outlines of my thoughts and should they meet with your approbation I doubt not I shall be able (if I am spar'd) to bring the woolen manufactory to a degree of perfection in a much shorter time than could be expected—But if the present proposed plan should not meet with acceptance [I] shall be happy to learn on what terms the State will give encouragement and if any ways advantageous, tho' not on my own plan will readily embark.

My reasons for giving the preference to Virginia are the western part seems natural to grass and the wool which I have seen growing in that part was good and might be greatly improved, provided there was proper encouragement given to the Farm they might grow wool of the first quality and in a short time be able to furnish the other States with Woolens—Should these rude proposals so far prevail on your Excellency as to obtain an answer, make no doubt but I shall be able to remove any scruple in my next respecting the possibility of bringing it to answer the most sanguine expectations—As the nature of this business in its

present stage will not suffer me to appear publick in it so as to refer
you to any House in America (tho' known) to be inform'd who I
am, but if I shall have any occasion to write on this subject again,
shall take care to send such a proof that will remove every scruple
respecting my abilities and such testimonies of my conduct that I
flatter myself thro' such a channel I can not fail in obtaining your
patronage, (which with God's blessing) I doubt not of success. I
have the honor to be Your Excellencys Most obedient Servant"

I've quoted this letter in full, not because it is especially literary,
but because it's a tour de force in how to suck up to a President
you have only met briefly once, and ask for state subsidy and land.
More than that, it is the attitude to enslaved people that is
fascinating. Howells clearly understands that the shortage of white
labour in Virginia, where Washington suggest he set up, means he
is going to have to rely on black labour. But far from proposing he
buys slaves outright, he wants to take on young people of colour
from slave owners who are considering emancipating their slaves,
offering apprenticeships from which they would be free after seven
years. I might be misreading this, but it seems like a sleight of
hand to offer indentured service that might to all intents and
purposes be tantamount to slavery. It might have made Howells
feel better to write in this way, but I don't imagine Washington
cared; slavery being legal in the US at this point and Washington
a slave owner himself.

Although the scheme was passed on to the Governor of Virginia
and approved in that state's legislature as an appropriate
programme for funding, the promoter of which was kept
anonymous, Howells' proposal ultimately failed. This may have
been because of the prohibition in England (and Wales) of
exporting machinery and skilled artisans to the US; a law that
should come as no surprise as the American colonies had only
recently been lost by the Crown, and we were not in the habit of
trading with our enemies. But this was not the end of Howells'
American pretensions as he visited Pennsylvania in 1808 to
research setting up wool manufacturing there, where he was likely
to have received a warm welcome from the Pennsylvanian Welsh.

Large scale immigration from Wales to the US had happened in
the late seventeenth century where a Quaker colony called the
Welsh Tract was established to the west of Philadelphia. A
hundred years later, the colony of Cambria, a present county

name in Pennsylvania, was established, and throughout the nineteenth century, Welsh people emigrated to work in and manage the state's coalmines. We get about. And not just to the more famous Welsh colony in Patagonia. When I lived in the US, it always gave me a thrill to discover things established by the Welsh, such as the now ghostly mining town of Bodie in Northern California, whose mines were run by the Morgan brothers from Cardiff. Their dark-eyed portraits stare at you in the preserved decay of the town museum.

Howells apparently took with him from Hay samples of his woollen goods and a letter of introduction to the Governor of Virginia. He was offered a large parcel of land near the Potomac, but declined, sold his goods for a legendary barrel of silver coins, no doubt an exaggeration of their worth, and returned to Hay as his wife was none too keen on leaving the town's home comforts for the so-called wilderness. His son however did leave for America in 1808, eventually settling in Ohio. And subsequent generations of Howells found fame as writers and journalists. His grandson was William Cooper Howells (1807-1894) and his great-grandson was William Dean Howells (1837-1920). William Cooper was mainly a newspaper editor and printer, and wrote Recollections of Life in Ohio (1813-1840), while his son was a well-known novelist, literary critic and playwright. William Dean was friends with Henry James, Oliver Wendell Holmes and Mark Twain, and in 1860 wrote Lincoln's campaign biography. Settling in Cambridge, Massachusetts, Howells wrote magazine articles for Atlantic Monthly and Harper's, half a dozen realist novels – the best known of which is The Rise of Silas Lapham – a volume of poetry and a children's book, as well as literary criticism. He was one of the first seven artists to be elected to the American Academy of Arts and Letters in 1904, becoming its president. Even if he is not read much these days, that's not bad, not bad at all for a Welsh boy with origins in Hay.

As for the fate of the woollen trade in Hay, the closure of Howells' mill was the end of its production. However if you want to acquire some Welsh woollen cloth, there is one place you can go. Up the back steps of St John's chapel in Lion Street, The Welsh Girl, is the studio and shop of Julie Leonard. Look for the Welsh wool woven bunting. Her limited edition collections of ponchos, scarves, bags and cushions are lovingly designed from traditional Welsh double weave tapestry wool cloth. In unrepeated and unique colour runs, they are the best way to wear a blanket. And they will last, well, practically forever. Welsh woollens are so strong they will keep for a century, or more of hard use. We still have a blanket owned by my maternal great-grandmother. Patched and stitched to repair moth damage, it is the best picnic rug I know. My Welsh Girl poncho in grey and pink, on the other hand, is something I hope to see my granddaughter wearing, after I've finished draping it over my knees, of course.

ENGLAND IN WALES!

An alternative source of Welsh woollens is The Great English Outdoors on Castle Street. Yeah, that's what it's called. I want to scream every time I walk past: We are in Wales! And this geographical inaccuracy, or if I am being mean, deliberate ignoring the very fact of Wales, rather puts me off wanting to buy anything from it, even though the offerings of home furnishings are lovely. Vintage and new Welsh blankets are available at proper prices, amongst leather goods, some great clothes and items for home décor. And the shop smells enticingly of beeswax and lavender. I'm glad I bought my Welsh blankets decades ago, though, as they have now become rather fashionable – I saw some tapestry woven ones in a very trendy interiors shop in Hoxton the other day – and with prices to match.

SOUTH

WELCOMING HILLS

Approaching Hay from the main Hereford Road, bear with me, I'm not having a geography fail, you can see the dark loom of the Black Mountains and the Brecon Beacons beyond from a dozen miles away. Their flat tops and sharp slopes are blue, grey, black and clothed in low cloud that moves quickly in this fast changing weather. Closer and they are green and black with patches of bare rock, rounded, smooth and gullied. Paths are visible from about five miles away. A low hill of wooded and pastured slopes rises between you and the Bluffs and Knobs.

The grass verges have been shaved one metre back from the road to leave wayside plants a chance. Ragwort, hogweed and nettles bully their way through daisies, knapweed and stands of dark pink rosebay willowherb, for me, the signature plant of the summer countryside. Hay is somewhere out of sight for now, though you can glimpse the river as a flash of silver between the beech and oak woods. A house martin is buffeted by the strong wind. The sky is the kind of colour fancy paint marketers call bone or ash, or something equally implausible.

Less than a mile into Wales and I am spiritually home. There are sheep in their pastures, wheat is ripening, and the hayfields have had their first cut. All the field boundaries are hedges, those important lines of green for wildlife to run under the cover of hawthorn, elder and maple. The farms are far apart and the main road is sometimes quiet for minutes. But back to the mountains.

CALL MY BLUFF

Hard core walkers trek up to Hay Bluff starting off somewhere in town and usually following the long distance footpath or National Trail, Offa's Dyke Path. I am not hard-core, nor to be honest much of a walker these days, so I'm driving on the Capel-y-ffin road south out of Hay. It doesn't take more than a few minutes until the road takes a sharp left hand turn at White Haywood Farm, where the farm gate choices are Morris' cider, firewood and eggs. The road skirts round the dark and tight packed conifers of Tack Wood, and at the next fork in the road goes right and on up the hill on a single track. I need to be careful here as it's high summer and there are a few townies around who don't know the width of their cars, or the etiquette of driving on one lane roads, or perhaps they just don't know what reverse gear is for, let alone how to or be willing to use it.

A few more minutes on and I am up above the treeline onto the open moorland that predominates the Beacons landscape. In the grass, bracken and heather wild Welsh mountain ponies graze

freely. I slow down to pass them at a snail's pace as they lift their black, or white and brown, or white heads to look at me with interest. Welsh mountain sheep compete for the rest of the grass around here. Several are dotted about. Later someone tells me there are ten sheep to every person in this parish. Someone else thinks it's more like thirty. At the stone circle car park, I swing my car off the road and look out over a more than one hundred and eighty degree view of the glorious rolling hills of Radnorshire, green in their clichéd quilt. Hay is hidden by the intervening hill I have just ascended. The Beacons stretch west as far as I can see, spur after spur of purple outcropped slopes. It's an astonishment. Wales is so beautiful, it almost catches my breath.

Taking one of the more obvious ways to climb Hay Bluff, I don my walking boots and head straight up the hill from the car park. It's a pretty tough steep walk. I am slow, but I don't care. Hill walking is not a competition. The well-worn and rather widely eroded path takes a zigzag up to the trig point. The Old Red Sandstone that makes up this part of the Brecon Beacons is quite open to the air here. I wonder about the kind of fossils that one might be lucky enough to find and recall, somehow almost impossibly from the deep recesses of my brain and a term of university geology, that the Devonian was the age of fish, ammonites and trilobites, amongst other things. The red of course is from iron oxide, and later I look up other nuggets about early sharks and huge forests. This is the sedimentary stone then from which many of Hay's buildings are made.

Six hundred and seventy-seven metres above sea level, Hay Buff is definitely a mountain. Anything over six hundred and ten metres (or two thousand feet in old money) counts as such in the UK. My American friends scoff at this, quite rightly. I remember for a moment that ridiculously titled and plotted film, *The Englishman Who Went up a Hill but Came Down a Mountain*, starring Hugh Grant, of all people. His character had to break the bad news to a Welsh village that their mountain was not high enough to be so defined. Unsurprisingly the villagers set about with buckets of earth and stone to make up the missing feet and inches. No such efforts are needed here.

Summer Moor

Newly bald summer sheep shield their faces from the rain,
turning towards lichened rock, they bleat for the sun.
The moor is a haze of heather and topiaried
gorse, sedges and springy moss. We raise skylarks

and scatter a small flock of goldfinches
from their blackberry feast. Incessant rain pours

down slate and thatch from sodden oak
and sticky sycamore soaking wall, rusting gatepost

like a nagging aunt who stayed too long complaining
about the tea being stewed and the scones unleavened.

Like many, I'm drawn to trig points, or trigonometrical points,
or triangulation stations, or trig stations, or trig beacons, or just
trigs; those odd structures atop hills and mountains used by
surveyors to measure and map the land. They are the goal of some
people's walking. Here small stones and a yellow wildflower have
been left on the plinth. A passing couple ask me to take their
photograph. They pose either side of the concrete pier as if they
have conquered Everest and I oblige. They thank me, adding a

neighbourly warning to watch out for the bees on the far spur, which is the apogee of my walk. I trudge on past the heather, noting the patches of exposed peaty soil, black and rich, and waterlogged. There are indeed bees on the cliff edge, but they don't annoy me too much. From my teenage beekeeping with my father, who was trying his best to live the good life in our suburban garden in Bristol, I know only too well that batting bees is the surest way to anger them. I ignore them. They soon realise I am not a nectar source and become bored with buzzing around my head. I find a likely step of grassy peat on which to rest and take in the view. Higher up, I can see so much further, and now to the east along the flank of Hay Bluff to Black Mountains and beyond. The green valleys of Hereford too are spread before me. It is at this point that I regret my organisational skills. No food. No water. It is a hot day and I am ridiculous in a summer dress. I enjoy the warmth of the sun for a good time, admire the young and fit backpacking their way across the moor and turn back to the path and the downward grind of my arthritic knees.

Hay Bluff is just one of the outcrops that make up the northerly edge of the Brecon Beacons National Park. Third of the Welsh parks to be founded, in its case in 1957, the others are Snowdonia (1951) and the Pembrokeshire Coast (1952). It stretches from Hay in the north as far south as Pontypool, and from Llanddewi Skirrid in the east to westerly Llandeilo. Five hundred and nineteen square miles of mountain, moor, lowlands, waterfalls and caves. The park is home to around 33,000 people, and attracts something like three million visitors a year, not all of whom are as feeble as me when it comes to walking, climbing, canoeing, fishing, biking and horse riding. It is a marvel, but please keep that to yourself. We don't want it turning into Cornwall: sky-high priced accommodation and lanes choked with traffic all summer long.

Over the hills a little away to the south lives one of Wales' well-loved contemporary writers. Owen Sheers, poet, playwright and novelist who has written of the beauty of this upland landscape too. In his first collection, *The Blue Book*[72], his poem 'When You Died', identifies the land as a source of consolation:

> I ran to the top of a hill
> and sat on its broken skull
> of stone and wind-thinned soil.

I watched the Black Mountains darken
and the river slip the grip of the town.

In his poem 'Skirrid Fawr'[73] he characterises that particular hill
as a horse. The mountain, like this poem is powerful, so powerful
that he is "drawn back to her for the answers/ to every question I
have never known." 'Farther' is another evocative poem from his
second collection when he climbs Skirrid again to catch: "the sky
rubbed raw over the mountains,/ us standing on the edge of the
world, together against the view". Quite so.

STARRY, STARRY NIGHT

Where I live in London I don't normally see more than about three
stars, Venus included, and that's on a clear night. Such is the
pollution of the night sky from the street and other lights of the city
that one of nature's wonders is all but lost to me. And it's easy to
forget that there even is such a thing as the Milky Way. I can
probably count on the fingers of one hand the times and places I
have actually seen it. I am so busy looking down and too much in
the city and indoors at night. It is a great reassurance and joy then,
to see that the stars are not only still there, but clearly visible from
Hay and the Beacons, if I just remember to go outside and look up.

The whole of the Brecon Beacons National Park is an
International Dark Sky Reserve to discourage light pollution and
preserve the star-spotting dark. The designation for the
outstanding quality of the night sky also has as its aims to reduce
energy consumption and protect our nocturnal wildlife. Other
such parks exist in Snowdonia, Scotland, and England. A drive up
to the stone circle under Hay Bluff has me at a good place to gaze
at the night sky, well away from the sodium street lights, only real
light pollution in Hay, and at which I could cheerfully lob a stone
or two. But patience is required. The stone circle is a bit of an
exaggeration, it might be marked as such on the OS map and even
have a name – Pen y Beacon – but in reality it is a disappointment
of four stones. Only one is actually upright, two are horizontal and
the remaining one barely puts its head above ground. And there
seems to be some dispute as to whether it is even a circle *per se* and
not perhaps a burial chamber.

The bright orange sun goes down under an anvil of cloud. In the gloaming I wait, watching mountain ponies making their way through the bracken. They are variously piebald, white, brown or black and this year's jittery foal is dark chocolate with a white stripe down its nose. Unmolested and free to roam, they are one the few remnant herds of wild horses in Britain. I put aside my asthma-inducing equine aversion for a few minutes to admire them from afar and the closed window confines of my car. Their snorts and snuffles are barely audible above the constant chorus of sheep; the sounds of the darkening sky.

I am no Patrick Moore or Brian Cox and have few star skills, which is where a handy phone App comes in to help me identify one pile of variously bright and distant burning rock from another. Sans telescope, I can name the basics: the Plough, Orion, the Pole Star, but after that I am prone to muddle up Arcturus with Betelgeuse, and as for tracing the sometimes far-fetched outlines of the zodiac signs, forget it. But I am patient and let my fancy take me across the sky in patterns of those sparkling lights that jewel the blue black. I could claim on occasion to have seen a shooting star, but this is a book not a Hollywood movie. Perhaps next time I'll try to improve my knowledge by booking a stargazing session with one of the park's astronomers contactable via the National Park website, or pick the brains of one of the park's fifty dark sky ambassadors. These are star spotting enthusiasts who run businesses in and around the park and who have been trained on all aspects of it and the Dark Sky Reserve, and are ready and willing to pass on this knowledge to visitors in order to enrich their experience of our wild places. I am content for now at having disturbed a barn owl from its fence post hunting perch on my drive home. The ghost of the fields is still haunting its patch. I found myself apologising to it, ignorant of whether my luck is now good or bad.

Christmas on the Beacons

This year I want to walk the hills
to a fresh dark –

a summit where I can wonder
on distant coastal towns
in their cliché necklaces
strung bright,

the Blues and Scarlets
switched on weeks ago to vie
with constant sodium.

And then I'll turn
to something darker –

the Sky Park is the only
beacon I wish for,
where far away points of light
have a chance to shine.

Years since I came here
for Hale Bopp; my compulsion
westwards behind a star.

LOOKING AT TIR Y BLAENAU
AND BEYOND

Here is the solid landscape of outcropped rock, hill, trees, made kinetic in the fierce wind, moving the whole. Dark clouds pass over the hill. The wide stream is massive, in full flood. Branches may soon be falling. The only fixed things living are three mountain ponies, two are unconcerned, grazing what can be found in the winter grass. There are no leaves, bar one of two brown hangers-on expressed in a wash of colour. The rest of the palette is black, grey, yellows and greens; limited and simple as it is winter. Even the stream is grey with black and brown ripples on the white background. And so David Jones' painting[74], made in 1924-5 while he was resident at Capel-y-ffin vivifies the high land south of Hay.

Approaching the Beacons on the cusp of winter, the leaves cling orange to the field oaks. The hedges have had their cut and are twiggy, exposing the ivy that overtakes them. Low mist covers the fields. A flock of gulls flies up into a copse, signalling in white. Crows fall from branches. The Black Hill is rusted from dead bracken. Visible now the gullies and runs frown its slopes. Hay Bluff in profile is purple, its downward slope a dry ski-jump. Frost crisps all the places of shadow. The car temperature gauge pings to tell me it is three degrees. I question the thickness of my coat. The very first thing I see coming into town on the Oxford Road is an enormous wooden Welsh dragon; a blast of fire, as when the national rugby team runs onto the pitch, and a huge statement: *croeso i gymru*. There's no doubt as to which country you are in.

The next morning it is one degree. There is snow on the high hills and delivery lorries coming from Builth have had to dig themselves out of the drifts. In town there is nothing more than frozen rain on the car, discs of ice cover the windshield. Blackbirds fight thrushes on the lawn, gold beaks against the spot and mottle. Hedge birds eat the buds of next year's leaves. The family who go swimming at 6.30 every morning set out in the dark and rainy end of night expecting a good day, not the full blast of winter. Their neighbours' boys were sledging at midnight in their pyjamas.

CAPEL-Y-FFIN – GILL SANS

In 1924 one of Britain's now most controversial artists came some eight miles south of Hay over Gospel Pass to the tiny hamlet of Capel-y-ffin to escape the mainstream. Eric Gill was in search of the spiritual and made his home in the monastery at Capel for about four years. Arthur Eric Rowton Gill to give him his full name was born in Brighton in 1882. He died in Middlesex aged 58 in 1940, having made his home at Speen near High Wycombe in Buckinghamshire on his return to England in 1928. Sculptor, engraver, essayist, printmaker and typeface designer, Gill was named Royal Designer for Industry by the Royal Society of Arts; its highest such award. Educated in stone masonry and calligraphy in London, he gave up his architectural training to follow these passions. He moved to Ditchling in Sussex in 1910 to start work as a sculptor. His work is in many collections, including that of Tate Britain, where at least two lovely wall carvings and one mid-sized statue, and can be found in the main collection on permanent display, and on buildings as diverse as Westminster Abbey, the Midland Hotel in Morecombe and the façade of BBC Broadcasting House.

Over subsequent years Ditchling became a Catholic artists colony where Gill, his wife, three daughters and adopted son lived; Gill becoming a lay Dominican. As well as working, Gill felt free to indulge his sexual passions, which, in no apparent contradiction to his faith, included several affairs, incest with his sisters and two eldest daughters, and sexual relations with his dog. These salacious details of his constant curiosity about sex were not known though until the 1980s or early 1990s, with the publication of his biography by Fiona MacCarthy[75]; and hence a controversial re-evaluation of his artistic reputation took place.

Life at Ditchling became difficult, complicated, competitive and far too public for Gill, hence the move to Wales. His time at Capel, as Peter Lord[76] explains, was one of Gill's most productive periods of work, during which he made drawings, sculptures and engravings, including such erotic illustrations to *The Song of Songs* that courted comment from his Roman Catholic friends, and the uncontroversial illustrations for *Troilus and Criseyde*. There are two gravestones carved by him in the churchyard at Capel and he also produced one of the most successful typefaces, ever. I see and enjoy the clarity of Gill Sans every day on the older London Underground signs and on Penguin book covers. Jonathan Miles[77] considers this typeface to be his greatest and most lasting contribution to art. He is less convinced by Gill's sculpture in comparison with contemporaries like Epstein, Brancusi and Moore. I can't but disagree. The bas-relief, 'Girl with Hair', is gorgeously carved, sinuous and lovely; the hair a river. In his typography Gill the artist meets Gill the socialist as, working with the Lanston Monotype Corporation, he produced a reasonable and readable typeface for universal usage; the exact opposite of the handmade notions of the elitist Arts and Crafts movement's private letter presses.

The habit of art principles of the community Gill organised at Capel afforded an opportunity to make work with an ecological awareness and care, as Miles explains. However the running of day-to-day life here was left predictably to Gill's wife and their daughters. Isn't it always? Always a woman somewhere with a broom and bucket. As Gill himself confesses in his *Autobiography* in praising his marvellous girls: "I, except perhaps in haymaking time, [am] no help to anyone, unless you call keeping a general eye on the whole show helpful." The family were constantly in need of funds. Living in the wilderness was a hardship, not just for the basics of daily life, but in the supply of raw materials for his work. Hauling stone to a remote valley came at the price of the carrier's cart. And there were other irritations. Gill records hoards of tourists visiting the monastery to see Father Ignatius' grave, and who would wander in and out of the bedrooms and ask to see a monk. John Rothenstein summed up Capel life on a visit in 1926 when he observed, as Miles reports: "Despite the constant rain, the damp house, the lack of hot water, lack of newspapers and Spartan food, …Gill's sharp-edged genial talk warmed the house."

Gill's clients were far from Wales and his own inclinations, as well as the necessity of visiting his London gallery owners saw him often away from Capel. Gill might have said Capel was a glorious, but strenuous life that he didn't want to leave, but by 1927 he was back in his studio in Chelsea working on the sculpture, 'Mankind', and only visiting Capel for a few weeks or even days at time[78]. Which is just as well, as in our current times it is hard to know quite how to write about him. Can and should one divorce the art from the artist? My literary training tells me that one should, the

biography is not that relevant, and no-one is seriously calling for 'Prospero' to be torn down from the walls of the BBC because of Gill's sexual predilections, any more than anyone seeks to ban Bryon for apparently sleeping with his step-sister. Yet the present and quite correct conversations on pederasty and its perpetrators make for this dilemma; one doesn't hear Gary Glitter's songs often these days. The passing of time seems to dull this, perhaps, not that I am for one moment comparing or conflating their artistic merits.

Half-Welsh artist and poet, and Catholic convert, David Jones (1895-1974) met Eric Gill at his earlier community of Ditchling in 1921, and, as Lord tells us, whilst not a disciple *per se*, he did consider Gill to be a great man. Engaged for a time to Gill's daughter Petra, Jones visited Capel-y-ffin, the chapel on the frontier, regularly and Wales "became the bond into the complex web of erudite mythological, historical and literary reference that informed his engraving, painting and writing for the rest of his life." Here he "sought to respond directly to the landscape and through that to the mythology" as Lord describes, as he genuinely wanted to connect to the land of his fathers – the Welsh thing. Even though Jones hailed from Brockley in south-east London, he signed some of his paintings with the Welsh spelling of his name. His time in the mid 1920s at Capel and on Caldey Island were the longest periods in his life that he spent in Wales. I can certainly empathise with these longings.

The paintings Jones made at Capel, included many watercolours, such as of Twmpa (or Lord Hereford's Knob), the next hill west from Hay Bluff, formed part of an exhibition with Gill at the St. George's Gallery, Hanover Square in 1927. Indeed Twmpa became a kind of motif for Jones – think Georgia O'Keeffe and Pedernal Mountain – so many times did he paint it in all kinds of weather and with all kinds of mark making. Jones' landscape work is generally un-peopled. Instead, in cases such as 'Capel Landscape' from 1925, the hills themselves have a bodily form, all curves and sexually suggestive rock formations. In other works the landscape and its rivers are in states of upheaval and disturbance. Stressed and disturbing, these are works where one can feel the weather and the movement of wind over the land. Criticised sometimes as unfinished and too loose, I find them exciting.

And he painted the Capel itself. Jones' engravings from this time include illustrations for Bible frontispieces, and commissioned works for books and poems such as *Gulliver's Travels* and *The Rime of the Ancient Mariner*. Thus the book influence here goes far back and invades the artist's work; engraving being the one medium that he seems to have learned much about under Gill's tutelage. Jones found the Gulliver project a dull one as it required too many images and he considered it a very boring book. Nevertheless the pieces he produced for the small boxes and rectangles that were required, are stunning. As a novice at copper engraving, the illustrations for *The Rime* proved to be a very great challenge for Jones, who confessed he was all at sea with the technical aspects of the subject matter. Yet, the work is lovely, even if, as his eyesight diminished, the end of its creation was on his doctor's advice, effectively the finish of his career as an engraver.

Like the rest of the Capel community, Jones found the life a strain, and the cold saw him often ill in bed. And he was troubled very deeply by his experiences in the First World War – he fought at the battles of the Somme and Ypres – however much he tried to make light of them. As to the poetry he wrote during his time at Capel, this was the beginning of this aspect of his creative life. In 1928, at the same time as he was working on the *Rime* engravings, he was beginning to write his first very long poem, *In Parenthesis*. Although not published until 1937, and nearly twenty years after the war that is its subject, this epic established Jones as a modernist writer, winning him the Hawthornden Prize. It was praised by W.H. Auden, who considered it a masterpiece, and T.S. Eliot, who in writing the poem's Introduction, called it a work of genius. Highly regarded at the time, the poem seems to have fallen from grace, as it is not a poem of the First World War that comes readily to mind, despite its influence being acknowledged by subsequent poets like Geoffrey Hill, Seamus Heaney and Simon Armitage. Owen Sheers, who these days is near enough to Hay to be called, without the usual pejorative overtones, a local writer, has done much to resurrect Jones' presence as a poet, for example Jones is the damaged artist of Sheers' novel *Resistance*, and a character in his play *Mametz*.

Even though the epic poem is focussed on the experience of war, there are passages using many influences from Wales, its mythologies and poems, and more specifically the border upland landscape. At one point Jones describes the Somme in specifically close to Capel terms: "The water in the trench-drain ran as fast as stream in Nant Honddu in the early months, when you go to get the milk from Pen-y-Maes."[79] Jones writes in his Preface "of the Celtic cycle that lies a subterranean influence as a deep water troubling under every tump of this island"[80] and of the Welsh element he goes on to say it "will only find response in those who, by blood or inclination, feel a kinship with the more venerable culture in the hotch potch which is ourselves", thereby very much identifying himself as Welsh. And his self-effacing apology, much like my own in the introduction to this book, is based on love. Jones quotes from Drayton's Foreword to *Poly-Olbion* where speaking of Wales he says "if I have not done her right, the want is my ability, not my love."

Jones returned from Capel to live with his parents, working, but also suffering several nervous breakdowns in subsequent years, disturbed as he was by the First World War. Thankfully he was spared military service in the Second World War as a result of this, but his life after the 1930s was a sad one of personal frustration with both his artistic and literary achievements, despite an Arts Council organised tour of his paintings in 1954, and his memorialisation as a First World War poet in Westminster Abbey in 1985. Not that he was around to see that. It was hard for him to work, haunted as he was by nightmares of the house being on fire.

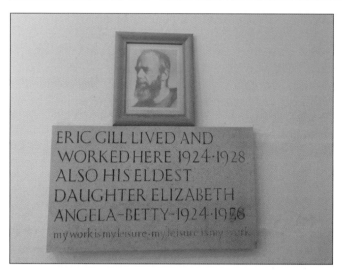

ERIC GILL LIVED AND
WORKED HERE 1924·1928.
ALSO HIS ELDEST
DAUGHTER ELIZABETH
ANGELA-BETTY-1924-1928
my work is my leisure·my leisure is my work

Surprisingly given his life experience there, the monastery at Capel was purchased by Gill in 1929 to be used as a school by his eldest daughter, Betty. It offered a wide curriculum to girls up to the age of fifteen, including such things as gardening and dairy work to all kinds of art and music to church Latin. Gill visited to teach drawing, and Petra taught spinning and weaving. The school failed and in 1936 Elizabeth Pepler opened the monastery as a guest house. Today it offers self-catering accommodation. The front door is helpfully left open for the passing curious to see the rather boringly dark portrait of Father Ignatius.

OUR LADY

I am sitting in St Mary's Church in town, waiting for the start of a piano recital, by the wonderful Daniel Martyn Lewis. One of his pupils, aged five, is sitting next to me. She is glowing with excitement to hear her teacher play. Shining down on us both is the banner of Our Lady of Capel-y-ffin. Out of sight for now is her side chapel, ablaze with candles. St Mary's is high church, the Anglican church in Wales, a hop, skip and station of the cross from the Holy Joes in Belmont Road, but why all this Marianism and why is there a huge white statue to the Virgin outside the monastery?

These days Llanthony Abbey[81] and the monastery is an inaccessible ruin as it was never completed due to lack of funds, and its domestic buildings a private home, but one is allowed to poke one's nose in the open front door and hallway to learn a little of its history. It was founded in 1870 by an Anglican lay reader who took the name of Father Ignatius. Kilvert describes the unordained Joseph Leycester Lyne as "a man of gentle, simple, kind manners, excitable and entirely possessed by one idea"[82], by which one presumes he means the foundation of a successful order of monks and followers. On an earlier occasion, observing two of the monks at work on the building, Kilvert comments on their garb: "It does seem very odd at this age of the world in the latter part of the nineteenth century to see monks gravely wearing such dresses and at work in them in broad day."[83] He clearly had a dim view of the revival of monasticism.

Ignatius' order's specific objectives were: i) the restoration of the ascetic life and continual prayer in the Church of England; ii) home mission work, by preaching, visiting the poor, and teaching the young; iii) to afford a temporary religious retreat for the secular clergy; iv) to raise the tone of devotion in the English Church to a higher standard by showing the real exemplification of the evangelical counsels; and v) to aid in bringing about the union of Christendom. There were three orders within the Community: the first, which fully observed the Rule of St. Benedict; the second was men and women leading a strictly religious life, using prescribed dress, reciting the canonical day hours according to the Benedictine use, and observing the five rules of the third Order, which was made up men, women and children bound by solemn

promise to obey five definite rules regulating: their attendance at the holy mysteries of the church; self-examination; the use of a prayer on behalf of the Society; the giving of alms; and obedience to the superior.[84]

Such stricture is so very far away from anything I can understand or sympathise with, and it was largely unsuccessful; Ignatius apparently attracted very few followers. But to answer my own question, report[85] has it that on 30 August 1880 a young monk called Father Dunstan saw the monstrance appear in the chapel, then certain of Ignatius' school pupils, four boys playing in the meadow below the monastery, saw Mary gliding across the surface of the field, and on three further occasions Mary was seen by the monks in a glowing light. Some visions then, including a glowing holy bush, if you believe in that kind of thing, but no miracles, or words of warning, or anything that might cause more than a handful of pilgrims to visit over the years, although in 1972 around 400 pilgrims attended a centenary celebration[86]. The Saturday before the August Bank holiday is the main day of pilgrimage these days, involving procession and prayers, including a prayer by Ignatius, but thankfully Capel-y-ffin is no Lourdes, with its hoards of holy tourists and sellers of tacky glowing sacred hearts, and pictures of the Pope on plates or on soaps on ropes. Thus the riding school pupils next door are left undisturbed.

OWLISH

It's awkward to drive down the U-shaped green of Gospel Pass in summer, the remote valley that seems to lead nowhere, as the passing places are a tight squeeze. There's been more than one occasion when I've ended up with scratched paintwork from too close an encounter with a hawthorn hedge. This is no short cut to Abergavenny. Today I'm visiting the chapel Kilvert thought looked like an owl. I'm not sure what he was on when he wrote that as I can only sort of see what he meant, but the small chapel of St Mary is none the less rather charming. One of the smallest in Wales, it measures a mere eight by four metres and was built in 1762 to ease church attendance for the more remote dwellers of the parish of Llanigon.

Capel-y-ffin means chapel on the border, which, if obvious, is nonetheless a fitting reminder of this littoral space. As Christopher Meredith explains and explores in what is becoming one his top hit poems, 'Borderland'[87]: *Ffin* is the Welsh for *border*. It occurs inside *diffiniad*, which means *definition*, and in Capel-y-ffin, a place in the Black Mountains:

> You'll find a ffin inside each definition.
> We see what is when we see what it's not:
> edges are where meanings happen.

On the black whaleback of this mountain
earth curves away so sky can start
to show a ffin's a kind of definition...

The church is about as far from a Georgian building as it's possible to get. Distinctly asymmetrical with its window placements and its rustic wooden paling into the porch, its wooden bell tower has slipped and is leaning at a frightening angle. Its slate roof is richly patterned with lichen and knobs of moss in all shades of green. The white exterior shows distinct signs of damp up the walls, and inside it is, of course, cold. But all is not totally miserable, come here any time and you can help yourself to a cup of tea or coffee. There's a kettle and plenty of supplies, so whether you're hiding from the blistering sun and looking for somewhere to cool off from the heat, or a place of shelter from the hail and rain, this is the spot. Just don't forget to dwell a while and drop a few coins in the box. Less wealthy than their English cousins, churches in Wales are always much in need of funds for their upkeep.

Had I been here in the winter of 1938, I might have seen an important guest of the cottage across the lane from the church. English painter, Eric Ravilious (1903-1942) came to Capel for a few weeks to work mainly on a series of watercolours. 'The Waterwheel' is a delicious picture with the Beacons in the background, expressed in shades of greyish green, skeletal trees stand on a bend in a stream, and several large and plump white ducks wait on the riverbank; they might be geese. The central focal point is the incongruous looking waterwheel. With similar strength of colour and stronger marks than many of Jones' paintings of the area, this is one to look out[88]. 'Wet Afternoon' has a figure walking along a lane in the village away from the viewer. It is a swish of wind and rain as he passes the partly bare winter hedges. The squat little church is in the background and the sky is busy in the rain. It has the same muted palette as 'The Waterwheel' and its same delightful energy. And in another of these works ('Duke of Hereford's Knob and the Chapel at Capel y ffin') the church is a creamy yellow with Twmpa in the background.

THE BLACK MOUNTAINS – A DAY OUT WITH GINSBERG, DELLER AND A BISCUIT

Another great October day in a run of beautiful warm-never-ceasing days, so it's surely a day to climb Twmpa, get up high and get some perspective. Lord Hereford's Knob is a peak on the Black Mountains right next to Hay Bluff. Titter if you must, I'm putting on my walking boots. Properly attired this time, I park below the mountain, next to the one other car there at the head of Gospel Pass. It looks like I am going to have the place to myself as there is no sign of the other car's occupants. The track is steep, but not muddy. I take my time and like the proverbial tortoise, finally reach the top, all six hundred and ninety metres of it.

The green, golds and reds of Radnorshire are laid out before me in the late morning sun. A wisp of remnant mist is making the view a little hazy in this season. The bracken has browned and keeled over. The heather is looking distinctly past its best. Nature is slowing down, yet the sheep are bleating away, a constant knell to the year, and high above me I fancy that wheeling bird is a buzzard. Autumn on the Beacons doesn't get much better than this.

And I am far from the only one who thinks so. In 2019 artist Jeremy Deller tried to claim the whole landscape of Wales from Hay over Gospel Pass to Abergavenny as his luxury when he appeared on Radio 4's *Desert Island Discs*. Not surprisingly he was denied, but he was granted a compromise; the road and the views from it. Lucky Hay folk have this access to this all the time and I doubt many consider it a luxury, though worth luxuriating in it certainly is.

I sit atop the escarpment for a long while, as my dog snuffles every possible scent there is, while I consider names and naming. I soon distract myself from mundane mentions, such as the satirical folk song of Lord Hereford's Knob featuring on the 2008 album, *Ambleside*, by Half Man Half Biscuit. So, when exactly did knob become, well, a knob joke? Later I do some digging. My old shorter OED tells me it's been the word for a hill for centuries, but is too polite to define the slang. Online I don't have much luck, so I can only assume that the nudge-nudge vulgarity is a much more recent coinage.

Calling

Cry cariad cry
to the soaring kites that rudder
above the escarpment and our heads.

Cry cariad cry
the chill wind through the bare
branches and onto our faces.

Cry cariad
for bletted sloes
and ripe rosehips.

Cry while we bask
however weak
the sun on our backs.

Allen Ginsberg didn't have any truck with this kind of consideration in his lovely 1967 elegiac poem for the natural world, based on a rainy/windy day visit to this very landscape. Part-Blakean in the lambs and symmetry, and packed full of sublime mysticism, it is pure Ginsberg. Read at speed and then with more consideration, *Wales Visitation*[89] is a hymn of praise and close ecological observation of the kinetic hills with which there is little point competing. It opens with:

White fog lifting & falling on mountain-brow
Trees moving in rivers of wind
The clouds arise...

and towards the end mentions the specific landscape we are looking at:

Heaven breath and my own symmetric
Airs wavering thru antlered green fern
drawn in my navel, same breath as breathes thru Capel-Y-Ffin,
Sounds of Aleph and Aum
through forests of gristle,
my skull and Lord Hereford's Knob equal,
All Albion one.

Ginsberg came to Wales that summer after participating at a conference in London (Dialectics of Liberation at the Roundhouse), hence his reflection on the distance he has travelled from the city to here. He escaped to the cottage of his publisher, Tom Maschler, near Capel-y-ffin for a few days, dropped some acid and engaged with the ancient land that had influenced Wordsworth, hence Tintern Abbey also making an appearance in the poem, as well as the landmarks closer to hand. One shouldn't take umbrage with his conflation of Wales with Albion though as I'm sure such sensitivities escaped him, so I'm giving him a pass on this. A detailed critique of the poem, noting its importance in Ginsberg's oeuvre, and its neo-Romanticism, by Luke Walker of Sussex University is worth your time and a few clicks[90].

Resisting the thinly-veiled derision of the host, Ginsberg later read the poem on an American TV chat show in 1968, explaining that it had been written under the influence of LSD[91]. If this project, as he called it, is writing on drugs, at least at inception, then I can only be very, very jealous, being too timid a type to follow suit. It is not surprising then that this wonderful piece was chosen as the title for and poem that guided visitors to the 2014 exhibition at the National Museum of Wales in Cardiff – *Wales Visitation: Poetry, Romanticism and Myth in Art*. Read it in full and you'll see what I mean; no illicit substances required.

Mountain Song[92]

is a sediment of solid words,
layering of ages in sand, mud,
chert; an accretion of Chaucer.

Norse fires its seams, and iron Angle clinks
and grykes them, Saxons them into synclines
of folded Norman with copper and lead,
and in Wales, the touchstone that is gold.

It is cut with crystal: Coleridge's streams
pick their way into caves of ice.
At its base all the frost and thaw
of Shakespeare makes treacherous scree:
a traverse for the sure-footed, the foolish,

and weathered rocks can shatter
from its summit with a rap and echo.

LLANTHONY PRIORY – SUCH A WINTER'S DAY

Cold and raining, it's the kind of day that epitomises the Welsh weather. A blanket of cloud has settled in over the hills and it's pouring steadily as I drive beyond Capel-y-ffin to Llanthony Priory. Tucked in the remote Ewyas valley, some fourteen miles from Hay, the priory is a romantic ruin left to stand, with current day intervention from CADW, since the Dissolution of the Monasteries in 1538. It's a good place for solitude at any time of the year. Today it's all water dripping from the thickly lichened Norman and Gothic stonework. I can see why Turner wanted to paint it, as well as, more famously, Tintern Abbey. His 1795 water colour in the Tate's collection[93] in its muted blues, greens and greys is all cloud, wind bent trees, rain and rushing water with the priory and its tower picked out in cream; the very definition of a sublime landscape.

A hundred and fifty years later, the ruins attracted another of our important landscape painters. John Piper stayed at Llanthony in 1941 to sketch and later create two brooding pictures of it in oils in his trademark chiaroscuro. They are now to be found in the National Museum in Cardiff and the National Library in Aberystwyth. Piper was brought here by a commission from the War Artists Advisory Committee and its project, Recording Britain. This was an attempt to capture in art the nations' buildings of historic importance, in case they were destroyed by the Luftwaffe. Piper did not restrict himself to the Priory (mistitled in the paintings as the Abbey, an easy mistake); he also made two paintings of the derelict cottages nearby.

A priory in this remote place was established originally in the very early years of the twelfth century by Walter de Lacy. The foundation myth[94] has it that out hunting one day the Norman nobleman took shelter from the weather, nothing changes there then, at an ancient and ruined chapel dedicated to St. David. Experiencing a Damascene moment, he decided to devote himself to solitary prayer and study. Later joined by Ersinius, a former

royal chaplain, and others, a church was consecrated in 1108. Within ten years, up to forty monks had taken up residence and founded Wales' first priory of Canons Regular, who lived together in a community, sharing property in common. They can be thought of as a sort of average between monks and secular clergy, not that I am especially bothered about this kind of thing, but it's good to know something of what the term actually means. Not exactly popular, for sixteen years they put up with attacks from the local population before retreating to Gloucester and their daughter cell in 1135.

Some fifty years later, Hugh, the fifth baron de Lacy, endowed the estate and started rebuilding the priory church, which was completed in 1217. In 1325 further building took place and a gatehouse was added. It is these buildings that form today's arched ruins. By the time of Owain Glyndŵr's campaigns in the early fourteenth century, the priory was apparently very much reduced as a religious house as its occupants retreated to Hereford and Gloucester. It was finally suppressed by Henry VIII with the remaining four canons pensioned off and the site sold. The buildings were ruined, but not totally destroyed, as in the eighteenth century the mediaeval infirmary was converted into the present Church of St David, and in 1799 the estate was sold. Purchaser, Colonel Sir Mark Wood of Chepstow converted some of the buildings into a house and shooting box. The present ivy-clad Llanthony Priory Hotel was Wood's house.

In 1807 poet Walter Savage Landor bought the estate and by an 1809 Act of Parliament was permitted to demolish some of Wood's buildings and, as part of his scheme to be a model country gentleman, erect a house, which was not completed. He planted many sweet chestnut and larch trees, still there and known these days as Landor's Larches. He also imported sheep from Spain and improved the roads. A friend of Southey, Landor wrote to him of the idylls of country life: all nightingales and glow worms. Such as they were, these idylls were short lived and Landor left for France by 1814, chased away by a combination of troublesome neighbours, non-compliant tenants, libel lawyers and the authorities, for which interactions he had prior form, and leaving his mother with his debts and the job of administering the estate until the Knight family acquired it in the twentieth century.

Landor (1775-1864) is worthy of a poetic detour. The Romantic poets' poet, he was not only a friend of Southey, but was acquainted with Wordsworth. I have to declare that despite my English degree, I was unaware of him until very recently. It seems he is being studied again as part of the Romantic canon, difficult though much of this might be as he wrote a great deal in Latin. He was a classical humanist, ranged against the age of industrialisation and is noted as an influence by Shelley, De Quincy, Browning, Swinburne, Yeats, Eliot, and Pound, who considered him the most important poet between Pope and Browning. He even inspired Dickens, who references Landor's relationships with his tenants in *Bleak House*, as in Boythorn and Dedlock's dispute over a gate. He is best known for a series of prose works, *Imaginary Conversations*, as well as epigrams and idylls, and numerous political writings.

Whilst in residence at Llanthony he completed his first significant collection of Latin verse, *Idyllia Nova Quinque*, which was published in 1815, and a contentious political piece, *Commentary on the Memoirs of Mr Fox*, of 1812, which was later suppressed by its publisher. His *Letters addressed to Lord Liverpool* of 1814 under the pseudonymous Calvus called for France to be stripped of all its territory acquired since the Revolution. In more pleasant vein, writing about the flowers of Llanthony,[95] he said: "I love these beautiful and peaceful tribes, they always meet one in the same place at the same season; and years have no more effect on their placid countenances than on so many of the most favoured gods." And elsewhere, Colvin tells us he likened Llanthony to a beautiful country or theatre for his meditations, which like Wordsworth, comprised walking, and walking on his own: "In this interval there is neither storm or sunshine of the mind, but calm and (as the farmer's call it) growing weather, in which these blades of thought spring up and dilate insensibly. Whatever I do must be in the open air, or the silence of night, either is sufficient, but I prefer the hour of exercise, or what is next to exercise, or field repose."

Despite this purple, his thoughts were sometimes far from beautiful and designed to barb, especially in his commentary of Fox's views on men, books and government where Landor's aim was to: "...represent his [Fox's] actions to his contemporaries as I believe they will appear to posterity...of all of the statesmen who have been conversant in the management of our affairs, during a reign of the most disastrous in our annals, the example of Mr. Fox, if followed up, would be the most fatal to our interests and glory." I dread to think what he would have made of our recent Tory governments and Brexit, but can easily imagine a vituperative tirade – a gunshot in words rather than the actual discharge of a firearm he apparently made when at Oxford at a neighbouring Tory student's window whilst Trinity College was at prayer, and which saw Landor rusticated.

Landor did not exactly look kindly on, or endear himself to, his tenants, and Colvin notes that he found the local Welsh folk churlish, malicious and un-improvable, and even more odious than the French: "If drunkenness, idleness, mischief and revenge are the principle characteristics of the savage state, what nation – I will not say in Europe, but in the world – is so singularly tattooed with them than the Welsh." Sharp intake of breath everyone. And a two fingered salute to Mr Landor from this Welsh woman. Savage by name and by nature, I suppose this is to be expected from an arrogant English landlord who sought and failed to stamp his idea of estate management on our wild country and ended up without sufficient funds to pay the interest on his mortgage. There is such a thing as karma and I imagine the folk thereabouts were rather glad to see the back of him, ironically to the Continent.

WEST

BRECON ROAD – WOODSTOCK

Driving east towards Hay from Brecon at the wrong time, you might easily miss the unprepossessing fields at the edge of town that for two weeks every year at the end of May and beginning of June are the site one of the world's cultural gems. Here in little old Hay, it's the Hay Festival. The festival moved out town more than a decade ago as it had grown just too much for its previous home in and around the junior school and other venues. Half of me thinks this is a pity as I always used to enjoy book browsing in between events, but now I'm content with doing so at the winter festival weekend in November, which remains in town. No, having the run of a huge site makes things easy for performers – no more sitting on green room chairs designed for children in a classroom – audience and organisers alike, and it's quick enough to get into town on the shuttle bus, not that all visitors do, which has affected trade in the bookshops and cafés. Stopping for a few minutes, I close my eyes at the empty field gate and recall the spectacle of white tents, and the multi-coloured banners, bunting, book-related sculptures, deckchairs, food and drink stalls, the huge bookshop, the whole wonderful mess of it. And the people; young and old from here and near and far away. All quarter of a million or more of them. And the talks and readings, music and comedy, spotting and listening to my favourite writers, finding new ones, and randomly challenging myself to attend an event the subject of which I know nothing, in other words to learn something new.

This is what Bill Clinton meant in 2001 when he called the festival 'Woodstock of the mind'. Probably the best tag line, ever, and no wonder it was been in constant use ever since. Peter Florence, the former festival director who lives with his family near Hay, tells me that was a pivotal year for the festival. Having booked Clinton, at no small expense, the festival was facing catastrophe when the foot and mouth epidemic struck. The decision was taken to cancel the festival, but the local farmers rallied round to man the closed footpaths, explain the situation to visitors, and supervise the footbaths needed to enable people to move about and for the festival to continue, thus cementing relations with town and country folk alike. People flocked to see Clinton, but were not so star-struck as to not provide the usual boo to someone who arrives late.

In its fourth decade now, having been founded in 1987 by Norman and Rhoda Florence with their son, Peter, using, as true legend has it, the proceeds of a poker game, its reach and depth is astonishing. The festival proper presents hundreds of events, in the form of mini-lectures, or book readings, or debates on subjects ranging from adventure to world affairs and everything in between. You can listen to poets reading from and discussing their work, and scientists explaining the implausibly difficult. And every year National Treasures like Michael Palin, Stephen Fry and Jeanette Winterson share the stage with huge names from the literary world worldwide, along with our well-respected journalists and our greatest politicians. Just take a look at some of the names who attended Hay in 2019: A.C. Grayling, Rosie Boycott, Marcus du Sautoy, Michael Morpurgo, Don Patterson and Arundati Roy – and those are just some of the names appearing on just one of the days.

I have extremely fond memories of listening to Terry Jones speaking on the disappearance of Chaucer from the mediaeval record and pointing the finger at his possible murder in an animated hour without notes and with great humour. Yes, it is true there is an element of celebrity spotting, by which I mean, seeking out my favourites from the grand dames and monsieurs of letters, and what is wrong, pray, with having Melvin Bragg sign a book for me? Internationally significant authors attending Hay in the last few years have included Toni Morrison and Margaret Atwood, but there's more to the spirit of Hay than promoting and selling books. Bigger though it may be these days with more than ten different reading and performance spaces, as Peter Florence told me, its core concerns are unchanged – our need as a species to tell stories, and to have a serious conversation. This is so even more now that it was thirty years ago. So audience questions and participation are key contributions to the conversation and debate, sharing the experience of reading in a community and with people who are experts in their fields, who have spent a lifetime thinking about their subject and may have written a few things about it too – books are the way we record what we know – and writers enlighten us all.

What continues to surprise and delight about the festival is its variety. About a quarter of the programme is dedicated to science, the environment and adventure. Organising it was, for Florence, a thrill: "in tracing lines of inquiry and adventure across genres and subjects, picking up on the threads of identity and dependence, of mistakes and reactions, of migrations and change, that run through fictions and poetry, through histories and scientific studies."[96] Attending is an exercise in empathy with the range of people and ideas and ways of seeing the world. Unlike a Hay chap I heard on the eve of the festival exclaiming that all hell was about to break lose, for me it's like stepping off my life for a few days and being in a better place, wishing things could always be like this. And I don't think that's just me. People return year after year, so there must be something in the water here. That or we all crave evenings of musical entertainment from well-known musicians to new discoveries, and being made to laugh our socks off by stand-up comedians.

Florence is a much-honoured member of the literary community. He was made a CBE in the 2018 New Year's honours list, holds honorary degrees from a number of universities to add to his own Cambridge one, including my alma mater, Glamorgan (now South Wales), is an honorary Fellow of the Royal Society of Literature, and chaired the Man Booker prize. As well as the never-ending task of running all those festivals, he found time to be a trustee for Hay Castle, and has edited anthologies and written a number of articles for the national press on topics such as censorship and freedom of speech[97]. I was sad to read of his resignation from the festival team in July 2021.[98]

The festival concerns itself with a number of projects outside the programmed events. Of huge importance is schools' day, the day before the festival proper begins, where the tents are packed with children enthusiastically listening to their favourite authors. I can only look at this with wonder and a certain degree of jealousy. How I would have loved this as a child – my inner bookworm set free. Another project is Hay Levels, pun intended, a series of filmed seminars on key topics in science humanities and social sciences by leading academics and permanently available on line[99].

Further, and to name just a few, there are development opportunities for Welsh writers under the Writers at Work programme to learn from the best during the course of the festival, and for one Welsh writer to be the Creative Fellow of the festival, attending all the Hay festivals worldwide to develop their own work and represent Welsh letters internationally. However criticism has been levelled at the festival events' lack of Welsh content. Richard Davies, writing in 2021,[100] whilst acknowledging fondly the importance of the festival to Hay, literature and his own life, reckons only four of the 138 adult events that year had any Welsh content. He bemoans the lack of involvement of Welsh authors and celebration of their writing. Perhaps, as he suggests, it is a result of the festival having gone on-line for 2020 and 2021 that it has come lose from its Welsh moorings and become in his words, 'Bloomsbury on Wye'. It's worth looking in detail at his observations. And let's hope things are rectified as and when we are able to gather again Hay in person to cheer, amongst other things, Welsh writing.

The festival does have to be well run; it pays fees, even if some writers choose to take those in wine or books, and it has to balance its books within the spirit of a co-operative. It also has a huge importance in the local economy. With a staff of twelve full time and five hundred at festival time, with five hundred more volunteers, its impact is estimated to be the addition of something like £26 million per annum to the economy within a thirty mile radius of Hay. Cultural and other pop ups appear all over the town at festival time ranging from sculpture and printing in the little church on Newport Street and in the garden studio of Tinto House, to shops selling sumptuous leather goods in the old Butchers shop, to gin and artworks in the former children's bookshop, to rare books in the King of Hay, and the Castle courtyard is full of street food stalls. Imagine then the impact of the corona virus pandemic. For the audience it was great that the festival was on-line and free to view in 2020 and 2021 (thank you to the sponsors and the government arts fund), but not so great for the town. I watched and enjoyed many, many events and I know friends who'd never had the chance to go to Hay were able to sample its delights. Many will make the effort to get there in person next time. But no audience to participate in the tourist economy represented a significant gouge to the town's finances. Government subsidies only go so far.

It doesn't stop in Hay. The festival team organise several international festivals every year as well in places like Mexico, Spain, Peru, Colombia, Denmark, India, and Croatia. These have reached over five million people over five continents. Quite some feat and not without its dangers. Florence has written about the competing demands of organising a festival in Mexico in the Noughties against the background of journalists being murdered, yet being petitioned by students and others to keep the festival open to allow a space for free speech[101], or the difficult decision of having to leave Budapest when the condition for continued government funding was agreeing to close the festival to Jewish and gay writers. Florence still ponders this decision: might it have been better to go ahead – part of the free speech remit being to allow persecuted writers to be heard – and risk the inevitable shut down? Controversy came to one of these international festivals in Abu Dhabi when a member of the festival staff accused Sheik Nahyan bin Mubarak al-Hahyan, the UAE Minister for Tolerance, of sexual assault in 2020.[102] Suffice it to say the festival no longer operates there.

And if you can't make it in person to any one of these festivals, then there's catch up. The Hay Festival has its own internet TV channel – Hay player[103] – which screens some selected events for free with most by subscription. No FOMO here, just more gratitude to the festival's generosity, and a very profitable way to spend many hours of screen time.

MY TURN

Being asked to read at the Hay Festival is a great honour, not that it has ever been bestowed on me, not really, not properly. Poets, poetry. Not exactly a huge crowd pleaser. But long ago, my best beloved, there was an afternoon in 2006 when I read to a small gathering of enthusiastic and supportive folk in front of the Welsh Books Council stand in the festival grounds. Their number included Sheenagh Pugh, a poet I admire hugely.

In the mid-Noughties a fine small press existed down the road from Hay in Rhondda Cynon Taff called Leaf Books. It published charming books of poetry and short stories small enough to be easily tucked into one's pocket. One such anthology was called In and Out of Love and it included one of my poems. Sadly, like so many before it, the press folded and went out of business in 2015. Nonetheless, I am grateful for my fifteen minutes of fame in the warmth and sunshine of Hay on a day when the cow parsley had grown to its full bridal veil height, almost obliterating the festival sign posts.

White Country [104]

From the bleached out sky
to the road's central line
and all in between – the blossom
on this month's hedgerow flowers,
the stellar stitchwort,
lane-dancing cow parsley,
and the trembling corona
of stamens on a plantain –
all is white blinding, new.

Rummaging in my portfolio and fingering the green advertising leaflet for the reading brings back a warm memory. I drove a long way for a minute or two in the bright light. And I did cheekily park in the artists' car park and walk into the festival through the artists' entrance and green room, which made me feel rather special. This is the short poem that for a brief time that year hovered in the air

above the festival fields and mixed with all the other words of all
the other writers:

My Krishna [105]

Your hair was always longer and wavier than my own
and when you washed it in the evening garden,

rinsing it with the scent of sundrops and nicotiona,
I'd swear the stars were reborn from its blue sheen.

You'd bring me fresh eggs, white shelled, saffron yolked,
and all morning we'd scramble in cool clean sheets.

At their most pungent, you'd snip green herbs and exchanging
daydreams we'd sip their balm in the geranium shade.

And when at night you left, as you always did,
your pillow was perfumed with mango.

THE MEADOWS – GIS A JOB

Turning left off the Brecon Road into The Meadows and Hay
starts to look like a business park. That'll be because we are at the
pill factory, more properly known as PCI Pharma Services. One of
the largest employers in Hay, the other being the Co-op at the
other end of town, it is one of the UK sites operated by this
American pharmaceuticals services company. It doesn't make
drugs per se, but rather it provides outsourced services to other
drug companies. In Hay, from its rather pleasantly landscaped
white and stone buildings, the staff provide drug packaging and
labelling services, and safe storage for drugs. This is more
interesting than it sounds, as when dealing with highly regulated
products like pharmaceuticals, great care needs to be taken in
providing the correct and controllable environment for
considerations such as light, moisture, temperature and so on.
Everyone now knows this in the context of Covid vaccines and the
conditions for their transportation and storage. Thus the facility

and the folk who work here are highly skilled, even though as many people point out, their salaries are not exactly the highest. But one should not be critical, this is a vital facility providing employment in what would otherwise be a very depressed area, and in recent years it has expanded its operations. It enables people to stay local, and that is to be lauded.

GYPSY CASTLE LANE – FIVE MORE WELLS

The tourist guide to Hay will tell you it is a town of wells, seven in total and it even speculates that the siting of St Mary's and St John's churches, within a triangle of wells, might be significant in a place already sacred to the Celts, sacred because of the wells. Perhaps there is something to this: Christianity building over existing religious practices as sites of worship or for healing. There are thousands of sacred wells in the UK, both springs and natural pools, and their uses are generally speculated to have been for cures for illnesses of various kinds from rheumatism to leprosy, obtained by bathing in their waters or drinking them, or for symbolic purification. Votive objects like scraps of cloth or pieces of metal have been found in or near wells, and there are stories of revelations being given to those falling into a dream state at wells. For all this mythology, whether you give it any credence or not, they are still sites of interest; there is something magical about watching water appear from rocks and listening to its splash and gurgle as it drains away.

Apart from Swan's Well down Gypsy Castle Lane, unless you go looking for them, the wells are rather hard to spot in Hay. Their mythology is noteworthy though.

In a garden next to St Mary's is Churchyard Well, whose waters were used for baptisms. Legend has it that a fire threatening the church tower was extinguished by a miraculous fountain of water that sprang up just when it was needed from the well. Ridiculous, of course, but one can imagine buckets being filled from the well, perhaps.

The Walk Well is behind St Mary's on the riverbank and is supposedly the place troublesome spirits could be laid to rest. How precisely this was achieved is not clear and what kind of spirits are we talking about anyway? A sprinkling of holy well water from the stone trough to allay someone possessed by madness is just about plausible, if not efficacious, but if we are talking ghosts and demons kind of spirits. Well, I'm stumped.

Eye Well is on the Bailey Walk very nearby. Apparently its waters have healing powers for all kinds of eye conditions with one proviso: the water has to be collected at dawn. There must have been a great deal of getting up early in Hay in days of yore for health and good luck for weddings.

The two other wells, which you really will have trouble finding, have been bricked up and are marked only by plaques on Oxford Road and Newport Street respectively. These are St John's Well and The Town Well. So much for seeking the blessings of the old goddesses of the land.

THE WORST VIEW IN HAY

Turning back up onto Gypsy Castle Lane after a hot walk along The Warren, I need to sit down and hydrate. Here's a likely bench tucked under the motte for my weary bones. The trouble is that, apart from affording close study of a bramble hedge, it has no view, in fact nothing at all to recommend it. It is an anathema in this place of fine vistas. Ah well, you can't have it all.

BAILEY AND NOT MOTTE

One of two parallel paths running from The Warren to Hay bridge, the Bailey Walk takes you closest to the southern bank of the Wye. The other path follows the disused railway. The path is not named, as one might be forgiven for thinking, after the nearby motte and bailey mound on Gypsy Castle Lane, but rather after a certain Sir Joseph Russell Bailey (1840-1906), Tory Member of Parliament for Hereford, Lord Lieutenant of Brecknockshire, and the first Baron Glanusk, who gave the land to Hay. Who he then? Lord of the Manor of Hay, he was part of a prominent South Wales ironmaster dynasty. His wife was the Lady Glanusk, who occupied Hay Castle in the 1930s. He was also the owner of Glanusk Park near Crickhowell, which is still today one of the largest private estates in Wales[106].

His grandfather, also confusingly called Joseph Bailey, inherited a share of the Cyfarthfa ironworks in Merthyr Tydfil in 1810 from this maternal uncle, Richard Crawshay. Over the Beacons from Hay in the heart of the industrial lands, Crawshay had built the works into the largest such in South Wales. It comprised of six blast furnaces, eight puddling furnaces, two melting furnaces, three balling furnaces and a rolling mill. For its time, in the 1790s, this was a huge complex and its success made Merthyr the iron capital of the world, and Crawshay an absolute fortune. Enough to allow his grandson, William, to build Cyfarthfa Castle, which is now the Merthyr Museum, and in the 1850s to extend, using, of course, an iron frame, a huge pile near London at Caversham Park in Caversham, Berkshire. I lived for a good number of years in Caversham – the place not the house. Until 2017 the house was better known as the BBC Monitoring Centre. I visited it once to read poetry for Anne Diamond on Radio Berkshire. Despite its later conversions into a school and by the BBC, it is still an impressive stately home.

I'm now going to claim a personal interest in this path. Bear with me, it's a bit complicated – history always is. My several times back maternal great-grandfather, one Joseph Gould, was the estate manager for the Crawshays. His office was in the fine Georgian building that today makes up part of the University of South Wales in Pontypridd, which is where, incidentally, my father received his tertiary education when it was a technical college – the former School of the Mines – and where, some fifty years later, I studied for my MPhil. It's hard to escape geographical destiny. There must be some magnetic force at play. Earlier, farming members of my mother's family, lacking the capital to exploit their iron ore deposits, apparently sold land to the Crawshays. Some of them went on to toil in the hell of the ironworks. Indirectly then, my forebears' labours earned their masters the riches to be able to gift the path to Hay. Knowing this, or at least, considering it as more than probable, makes me enjoy every step I take along the path all the more. I'm reaping the fruit. Thank you, family all.

These days the Hay Woodland Group undertakes much of the maintenance of the path, supported by cash from housing developer, Persimmon, and has commissioned some new additions. As damaged and fallen trees are removed, their stumps are retained to stabilise the riverbank and part of their trunks have been turned into chain-sawn sculptures. First there was a fox and an owl, then a buzzard and an otter and so on. High art they are not, but they are rather charming all the same – don't look at the join where the trunk was removed and repositioned for ease of carving – and children love them.

MORE GOD STUFF

Down Gypsy Castle Lane and I reach St Mary's Church[107], the Church in Wales one, even though if bizarrely I've seen the Cross of St George flying from its flagpole, and no it wasn't on 23rd April. It is about as Catholic as you can be as an Anglican without actually being a Catholic. So, that'll be a waft of incense on a Sunday morning. Given that it's not exactly my scene, the only thing that might actually attract me to sit through a service, is the fact that I can bring my dog. Dogs are not only welcome, but positively encouraged. Still, what I am rather more interested in is the building.

Building churches near the castle was the norm, pun intended, in the twelfth century, hence it's hard by the motte and not the present castle. Over the centuries the building suffered at the hands of absentee vicars and churchwardens, having largely collapsed in about 1700. In 1827, the latter were summoned to the church court in Brecon to explain their neglectful selves.

Luckily the building was saved by a wealthy curate, Humphrey Allen, who came to Hay in 1825. The church was largely rebuilt in 1833 under Allen in late Georgian gothic style in blocks of grey sandstone. He largely did away with the proprietary pews to enable many more free pews to be available to worshippers. The church continued to be well looked after by Archdeacon William Lathan Bevan, resident of the castle and the first resident vicar St Mary's had had in over a century. He ministered to the residents of Hay for nearly sixty years.

The only original parts of the church are the tower and some eighteenth century grave slabs; previously in the floor of the nave, these were re-sited to make outside paths. There is only one bell, which came from Chepstow in 1740. Apparently there were six previously and they were sent away for repair and recasting, but did not return. Legend has it they are in a watery grave on the bed of the Wye in Steeple Pool, just beyond the church.

Things worth looking for inside include the very badly worn figure reclining at the west end, which is not Maud or Matilda de Braose, as some people romantically mistake it, but a monk of unknown identity. The pulpit was paid for by a Dr Trumper in 1865 in memory of his wife. It is a finely carved Italianate alabaster affair. The carved screen is rather grand. The icon of St George was painted by artist and signwriter, Christina Watson in a traditional orthodox style. But most outstanding is the organ. Installed as recently as 2010 and at vast expense, it was build in 1883 in London by Bevington and Sons and belonged originally to John Carbery Evans of Hatley Court in Cambridgeshire. It spent its life in various country houses before coming to Hay via Homer Church in Hereford. Its beauty is not only its resonant sound, but its gilded light oak case. Played by the current parish priest and music scholar, Father Richard Williams, it attracts

performers of organ music from far and wide. The nineteenth century blue and white Stations of the Cross are a similarly new addition.

Maudlin though it is, I rather enjoy wandering around graveyards. There is something of the residual Goth in me. I'm not usually looking for flying bats, and I certainly wouldn't want to encounter anything inexplicable, so I keep my perambulations between the mighty and ancient yews to the daytime and to where grief is a weeping woman draping herself over an urn. What is fascinating is the style of and dates on the stones, and what their inscriptions tell you about the dead. It is the raw material of potential stories for any writer. As a child and again with my own children, we used to hunt for the oldest grave in any churchyard we passed. In St Mary's yard this is dated 1697. The problem with trying to glean much from the gravestones here is that the local stone used in carving them is very crumbly, so much of what was written is now lost. Thankfully Bryn Like made a record in 2016[108]. He noted the occupations of those buried before 1870 and those whose ashes have been interred since as: 17 Inn Keepers; 13 'Reverends'; 9 Surgeons and 9 Builders; 4 Saddlers; 3 each of Boot & Shoe Makers, Drapers, Butchers, Maltsters, School Masters & Blacksmiths; 2 each of Jewellers, Bankers, Mercers, Woollen Manufacturers, Coopers, Grocers and Ironmongers; 1 Land Surveyor; Plumber; Carpenter; Mason; Joiner; Cabinet Maker; Wheelwright; Currier (leather worker); Timber Merchant; Hatter; Estate Agent; Painter; Excise Officer; Glazier; Hairdresser; Postman; Plasterer; Glover; Army; Navy; 'Gent' and scotchman (travelling salesman). In some ways an unsurprising list, in others it is rather telling.

MORE DEAD PEOPLE

Cutting back to the Brecon Road, and in grave mood, I visit Hay Cemetery, where less ancient, but still magnificent, yews have been allowed to grow into one another forming an archway at its centre. There are a few notable graves here making the detour worth the time spent. Many folk from hereabouts reached their centenary, which is increasingly less remarkable. One imagines the Queen's office being rather busy sending congratulations cards these days.

Archdeacon Bevan's grave of 1908 has an elaborately carved Celtic cross; five different knot patterns twist their decoration over it, resisting the thick lichen that is doing its best to obscure them. The verdigrised bronze fallen Icarus with his broken wing is twenty-four-year-old Pilot Officer Lancelot Steel Dixon of the RAF. He was killed in 1940 on the day he earned his wings. Making an official map reading flight into a celebratory one over his parents'[109] home, Clock Mill at Clifford, he lost control of his acrobatics, or his Harvard plane malfunctioned, and he went down in flames in a field near Hay. I can't imagine how his parents' joy turned to horror. What an awful accident. No wonder his sculptor mother, Christina Goad, wrote *mater luctuosa fecit*[110] on the touching life-sized tombstone she made for her beautiful boy.

Among the seventeen war dead, easily spotted by their super-clean cream stones, is a curiosity. Besides the British and Italians, there are ten German graves. These prisoners of war died in the military hospital down the road from Hay at Talgarth. Many of them died after the cessation of hostilities, and one of their number died in 1948, three years after the war ended. Saunders relates the possible theories as to why he and his fellows were not repatriated.[111] Thirty-seven year old Max Pfefferkorn may have wanted to remain in Wales, or he may have been a less desirable German: Nazi party members or those of the Waffen SS were detained by the British for far longer than so-called 'good'

German POWs. Who knows? The truth now rests with Max and the others in their graves.

And to add to our catalogue of professions we now have, of course, a bookseller. (John) Geoffrey Aspin was a collector of texts of and on French drama, and was seller of all things related to French literature, history and thought. Especially active in Hay in the 1970s and 80s, his shop was at 27, Castle Street.

THE WARREN – LIFE'S A BEACH

The path down to The Warren from Gipsy Castle Lane is stony and dusty, the nettles are head high and brambles have grown almost to its middle. The lane has been patched with broken concrete and rocks and is a treacherous drive for one's car axle. That's why it's better to walk. The car park at the end of the single track is tiny and on a baking summer's day is always full. There's always one idiot who thinks a passing place is a parking spot despite the notices advising the necessary right of way for agricultural machinery. Why are there so many entitled fools around? Don't answer that.

Across the meadows to the river, there are no rabbits of The Warren's name bred here now for the Lord of the Manor's table, but the grass has had its first cut. Enormous cylinders of hay dot the adjacent field. One final week in nature's drier and its off to the barn with them. At a bend that cannot really be described as a meander, the Wye here is beached by stones that can accommodate tens of people. The riverbank is partly shaded and flat, and the river clear and wide. Opposite is a high cliff of red sandstone, a clear attraction for young climbers of all kinds, however inappropriately kitted out. Sometimes it looks like an accident waiting to happen. All the more reason for keeping the car park gate clear for emergency vehicles.

Canoes float by paddled with various degrees of competence. The water in high summer is almost warm and most importantly deep enough to swim in. This is without doubt the best place in Hay to cool off on a hot day. The usual rules apply to not letting on though. An afternoon of alternately dipping and drying off, swimming and sunbathing, reading and minnow spotting is an afternoon for the soul well spent. Dogs love it. People of all ages love it. And it is thanks to the Hay Warren Trust that we can, as it bought the land in the 1970s to save it from becoming a campsite. There are plenty of those in Hay's environs in any event.

CASTLE STREET – GOLD POST

At the top of Castle Street, and easily missed if you are staring into shop windows, is something rather glittery and special – a gold post box. I've never seen one of these before, but here in Hay there is much glister. It was painted by the Post Office to honour the gold medal winning Cusop resident and champion discus thrower, Josie Pearson, after her triumph at the 2012 Paralympic Games where she set a new world record. Pearson is deputy mayor of Hay these days and has been influential in re-visioning access to Hay for disabled people, and pushchairs. The town's Shared Access Plan has funds from Natural Resources Wales, and Hay is in the process of building a five-mile-long accessible trail around the town. This involves replacing stiles with gates and enlisting labour from volunteers and National Park staff. And there's more; the town council has audited access to Hay's shops and other buildings, providing, so far, nine portable ramps to the buildings, as opposed to the businesses. I don't expect the planners of the Olympic legacy could have imagined this, but here we are nearly a decade later with a foresighted council opening up the town to those with mobility issues. Hurrah for that. Inclusiveness is one of the really good things about Hay.

BEYOND

BREDWARDINE – QUICK NIP OVER THE BORDER

It's a cold spring day, in between April showers that are about as benign as a January storm – hail, sleet, snow even, and I've decided to leave the country for the day, meaning I'm driving a few miles east of Hay past hedgerows frothing with blackthorn to the village of Bredwardine. Tucked on a meander of the Wye and pretty though it is, there aren't many reasons to come here. I have something particular in mind: a pilgrimage, of sorts. I've come to say thanks to Francis Kilvert, who has guided some of this book.

Kilvert left Clyro in 1877 when he was made vicar of St Andrews at Bredwardine. The incumbent for only two years until his early death from peritonitis – nasty, he died only a week after returning from his honeymoon. He is buried in the churchyard he describes: "The southern side of the churchyard was crowded with a multitude of tombstones. They stood thick together, some taller, some shorter, some looking over the shoulders of others, and as they stood up all looking one way and facing the morning sun they looked like a crowd of men and it seemed as if the morning of the Resurrection had come and the sleepers had risen from their graves and were standing on their feet silent and solemn…"[112]

His grave is a plain cross on an unadorned series of plinths, elevated like a preaching cross. It's simple and appropriate, but it doesn't say much about the man or the riches his diary has left us as a charming social history of Victorian rural Britain. I was hoping for something more than these two perfunctory quotations from the Bible: "Until the day break, and shadows flee away", and "He being dead yet speaketh". Hey ho. I resist the temptation to place a pen on his grave. This is a cliché too many, even for me, and is best left to the hoards of devotees who visit Sylvia Plath's grave in Yorkshire, where a veritable stationery shop clogs the grass. I leave him a few daffodils, and one writer to another, nod my head.

The wind chases me into the ancient Norman church with its kink in the nave. The mediaeval tombs of two members of the Baskerville family are interesting, but some days, you've seen one recumbent knight, you've seen them all. No, what draws my attention requires me going outside again to the red sandstone carved lintel over the blocked up north door. Within two cross hatched columns are two eight leaved circles. In alcoves in the middle are two carved figures. These are hard to decipher and interpret. One looks like a bear tied to a post. But most people think it is unidentifiable. Even squinting, I'd have to agree. The other is of more human form. Even though one commentator thinks it is a monkey and you can't even tell its sex, I beg to differ. It looks female to me – big clue, it has breasts, and a fancy hair style or headdress. And it has its legs open. I'm pretty damn sure it is a Sheela-na-gig. What she?

Female figures with exposed vulvas, Sheelas are mostly found carved on churches in Ireland, the UK, France and Spain. They seemed to have originated about a millennium ago. [113] Their unrealistic and grotesque forms are thought by some to represent female lust as hideous, sinful and corrupting: a warning to the congregation, and as usual women coping the blame for inciting men. Sigh. Some things never change. The other school of interpretation [114], and which is much more appealing to me, is that they are depictions of ancient fertility or mother goddesses: the female equivalent of the green man, and a lot more exhibitionist. Old hags, or not, I rather like their unabashed display. They are one in the eye for religious morality, and capable, some say, of repelling evil spirits.

With these pagan thoughts, I leave Bredwardine and take the long way back to Hay via the hill to Dorstone. There's something even more ancient in this landscape with which I want to spend time communing. Arthur's Stone is a five to six thousand year old Neolithic chamber tomb. Its slabs are huge megaliths, and even in their partly collapsed state, it is still awesome. As always, one asks, how on earth was this built – moving a twenty-five tonne capstone onto its upright supporting stones and earthing up the whole, and why was such an effort made to bury whomever it once contained? Shivering on a windy hill, though I am, and with icy rain in my face, I am having the full ancient upland Britain experience. I need to come back another day to wonder about its use for ancient ceremonies and worship, or even just to admire the large whorls of lichen that decorate it.

ST MARGARETS – GOLDEN DAY

Another season and another foray into England beyond Dorstone, driving south through the Golden Valley, I am in search of treasure. The valley was beloved by C.S. Lewis apparently, but today I am travelling in the footsteps of another of our twentieth century writers, poet laureate, Sir John Betjeman. I'm no admirer of his poetry with all its thumping rhythms and rhymes, as to my contemporary ear they are too much, with the exception of his playing tennis with Joan Hunter-Dunn or wishing to annihilate Slough. Perhaps, his legacy now is as a supporter of our railways and lover of our churches. As I progress some twelve miles south-east from Hay and with the birds all safely fledged, it's hedge-cutting time. Every contractor is out with the machinery that spits random leaves and twigs on to the slow-going give-way roads as the hedges are cut to within an inch of their lives, leaving so many damaged and bare branches it's a wonder they manage to regrow at all, but somehow they do.

I've been tipped off by a fellow I met along the way, who spent lockdown one in St Margarets. Thus I've come to the hard to find, out of the way church of the same name. A one-track road leads to the squat building with its wooden bell tower. Dating from the twelfth century, it looks like your average ancient church set in a grassy plot of ornately carved and crumbling tombstones made of the same sandstone as the church and thickly encrusted with lichens. These are surrounded by harebells, thistles and coltsfoot that dance in a warm breeze coming up the valley, over which there is a magnificent view. The yard has become a wild meadow with a few paths mown through it. Yarrow, plantain and clover are more lovely than the commercially grown flowers left on the graves. It's been a wet summer and marvellous for our native plants.

Step through the heavy wooden door though and I defy you not to gasp. The breath-taking treasure here is an exceptional rood screen and its loft, complete and unharmed by Henry VIII's orders in 1547 to do otherwise. The oak screen dates from 1520 is beautifully carved all over with foliage that makes it look like lace. The bosses have heads, lions, knots, shields and so on. Richly painted and gilded in its day, it was restored in recent years to its current lime washed appearance. Sit and dwell on the skill of the wood carvers, but not on the eighteenth century texts write large on the walls of the church, especially the one over the door suggesting that you 'Go and sin no more.' Here's Betjeman writing on it:

My own memory of the perfect Herefordshire is a Spring day in the foothills of the Black Mountains and finding among the winding hilltop lanes the remote little church of St Margaret's where there was no sound but a farm dog's distant barking. Opening the church door I saw across the whole width of the little chancel screen and loft all delicately carved and textured pale grey with time.

It is quiet and out in the churchyard all I can hear are the birds and the furious buzzing of bees, which have made their home in the eaves above the altar. There's no barking dog today. The Black Mountain looms to the west, an insistent presence of adventure and danger. It calls me home with views of its sharp blue north-facing slope like the lines on a graph, the kind of Covid infection statistical trend we wish for on a daily basis.

CUSOP – HOME VIA HOLLYWOOD

Turning into Cusop Dingle, I take another detour as far as it is possible to drive. The large Victorian houses – gentleman's residences you might call them in estate agent speak – that make up this village on Hay's south-easterly outskirts, just over the bridge of Dulas Brook and into England, were once home to notables such as the so-called Hay Poisoner, and the Booth family. Unless you enjoying hedge peeping at large piles, and hands up, yes, I do, there's nothing much to make you go to Cusop. And the dingle is not exactly welcoming, making it very clear that there is no turning for vehicles the further you drive along it. This is not actually true, but I imagine it keeps away the more law-abiding amongst the passing motorists.

Cusop church[115] is worth stopping for. Another lovely Norman church, St Mary's was originally dedicated to the sixth century St Cewydd. Welsh saint of the rain, like St Swithin, his feast day is 1 July, and bad luck for our summer if it rains on that day. Inside is a cross hatched Norman font – saltire crosses to be precise – the memorial to poor William Seward – the Methodist preacher who was stoned outside the Black Lion – and a beautiful new stained glass window for the Millennium, designed by stained glass artist, Nicola Hopwood[116]. There's something really heartwarming about new works of art being commissioned by churches: the continuation of a tradition, and demonstration that they are more than historic places preserved in aspic, but part of a living community. You might think of the more grand and expensive, such as Anthony Gormley's Monk in the crypt at Winchester Cathedral, or David Hockney's Yorkshire spring window in Westminster Abbey, but Hopwood's window here is a smaller and no less joyful an example of this trend.

And there's more: the church's treasures include a Welsh prayer book from 1664, and the churchyard is beautifully maintained and has some interesting gravestones – the contemporary one for Richard Booth's mother, Catherine, is of the sort of design that I rather fancy for myself: simple but pleasing. The four other things worth pondering are the ancient yews. Their thick reddish trunks – one has a girth of over thirty foot – evidence their age and symbolise centuries of worship on this spot: not all of it Christian perhaps, as these yews, sacred to the Druids, are thought to be as much as two thousand years old. Just let that sink in for a moment.

Yew

Guardian of peace
yet its berries tempt
a succulent death.

For longbows its wood
is battled hardened.

Our future contingent
on this secret cache
of green fringes.

As to other ancient beliefs, Cusop can lay claim to tales of faerie folk. It is reported by Ella Mary Leather in her The Folklore of Herefordshire of 1912, that local people recalled seeing faeries dancing under the foxgloves in Cusop Dingle. For a moment images of those Victorian fake faerie photographs pass in front of my mind's eye – cute, but obviously unconvincing. If not tiny people dancing in the late spring green, then there are tales in Leather's book of impish brownies sitting on pot sways over fires and doing who knows what to one's repast. Darker still, there's said to be a meanly dressed old lady on the Black Mountains who leads travellers astray. Nonsense all of it, of course, but charming in its way. All the same, you won't catch me walking the dingle or mountains after dark.

WHITNEY ON WYE – PRICE ME A RIVER

One of the other ways to get to Hay from England and the east is to turn off the A438 just after Whitney on Wye and take the toll bridge[117]. There's been a river crossing here for two hundred and forty years, give or take. Before the bridge, using the ferry, or one of five or six fords between Whitney and Hay was the only way to traverse the river. The present and fourth stone and timber bridge was built in 1798, high enough above the water to avoid its floods. Its history is completely commercially driven.

As a result of pressure from local farmers with grazing land on either side of the river, and with the commercial carriers from Hay and Hereford finding the ferry of insufficient capacity and convenience, its owner, Tomkyns Dew agreed to petition Parliament for the construction of a bridge in 1773. The bridge scheme's supporters, or undertakers, were given sufficient land to build the bridge and toll house, taking the materials *gratis* from Dew's land. In addition, Dew had to be compensated for the loss of his ferry income. However, the hurriedly-built and poorly sited first, second and third bridges were severely damaged by the under-estimated power of the floodwaters of the Wye. In 1796, application was made to Parliament for a stone and timber bridge by a new group of promoters from Hereford and Hay. Thus the current structure was devised and erected.

Though the historic toll list makes interesting reading as to the forms of transport, the new tolls cover cars and commercial vehicles, with certain exemptions for public service workers and the military. Cycles are free. One allowance that caused resentment for some fifty years, apparently, until the mid-nineteenth century was that which exempted the original landowner, Dew's family, heirs and servants, and any future owners or occupiers of the Mansion House at Whitney Court, along with anything they might want to carry across the bridge that might conceivably be the subject of a toll, like horses and cattle, carriages and dog carts. So much for entitlement.

And on goes the history of making money from the bridge. Against competition from the horse drawn Brecon to Hay to Eardisley tramway, which started in 1811 and wanted its own bridge, the owners were able to retain their exclusivity to the river crossing and charge the tramway for using the existing bridge. When the railway came from Hereford to Brecon in 1859 and needed its own much stronger bridge, the bridge owners were guaranteed a certain level of toll income by the railway company as compensation for loss of traffic. Even today, the owners of the bridge are granted their toll income tax free by virtue of the relevant Act of Parliament. They are obliged to maintain and upkeep the bridge, of course, which is no mean feat, but it is some exception.

As well as a convenient crossing point, a tourist business has been developed around the bridge. There's a campsite, canoe launch, café, and eco-lodges to stay in. It's become what in modern parlance we call a destination, complete with an invented troll called Walter, who has his own children's book. Although not somewhere I would want to spend a time, these are the necessary steps that have to be taken to make a living and recoup a huge investment, one presumes.

There is something rather distasteful to my mind about the continuing notion of private ownership of roads and bridges. Representative of quaint British eccentricity and a quirk of our national heritage they may be – Grade II listed in this case – I'd still much rather no infrastructure rested in private hands, even here in out of the way Whitney. It's a surprise that it survived when Hereford County Council adopted all the other toll bridges in the 1920s, but survive it did, and it has been privately sold multiple times during the last hundred years.

When I lived in Berkshire, it used to irk me greatly that I had to pay a toll to access Pangbourne from the north bank of the Thames. All I wanted to do was walk the dog and children along the water meadows, and yes, I know it was only 40p or whatever, but it's the principle. I already pay to use the roads in my general taxes, council tax and vehicle licence duty, so enough already. You can imagine then how annoyed I felt about paying to come into my own country over one of the Severn bridges. Thankfully that is over and done with. But we do have to suffer an unfortunate name change. That's the rub for the republicans amongst us, which in my family is all of us, as we simply don't do the royals. Like all those who objected to the new nomenclature, I cringe at every crossing of the Prince of Wales Bridge. It is no surprise then that its horribly expensive signs – nearly a quarter of a million pounds if you please – have been defaced. I hope it won't be long before they are taken down.

The same annoyance rises in me when I am travelling to Hay, which is why I keep on driving and take the free bridge into town from Clyro. Like choosing, or not, to take the M6 toll, or pay the congestion charge in London, at least there is an option here. On many of the twenty or so other toll roads and bridges in the UK, there really is no alternative. And that is all the more galling.

CLIFFORD – ROSE OF THE WORLD

A small village four miles to the north of Hay, and in England, Clifford has a few claims to fame; most notably its now ruined castle was home to one Rosamund Clifford (c.1150-1176). Fair Rosamund or Rosa Mundi was the mistress of Henry II and supposedly the love of his life. Daughter of lord of the castle and Marcher lord, Walter de Clifford, she was educated at Godstow Nunnery near Oxford. The various legends that surround one of the beauties of the twelfth century is that her trysts with the king took place in the secrecy of the maze at Woodstock in Oxfordshire. The Queen, Eleanor of Aquitaine, is said to have confronted Rosamund in the maze and offered her the choice of a dagger or a cup of poison. Rosamund took the latter and died in a scene that was centuries later depicted indoors by the Pre-Raphaelite, Edwin de Morgan in 1878. His painting has Rosamund with roses in her hair and surrounded by putti and doves cowering before an evil looking Eleanor, who is shrouded in the night sky and holding a glass of red liquid. The stained glass window above Rosamund shows two lovers kissing and the maze is visible from the doorway. It is a dramatic fantasy in storage at the De Morgan collection, but available to view on-line as the fancy takes you.

Multiple different tales were embroidered about Rosamund, her relationship with the king and her fate at the hands of the queen, or not. I doubt she was roasted between two fires, stabbed by the queen and left to die. Still, there are few royal mistresses who have sparked the creation of so many English language, French, German and Italian poems, ballads, stories, operas and paintings. Just a sample of these include: Donizetti's *Rosomunda d'Inghilterra*, Apollinaire's *Rosemonde*, novels by Susan Howatch and Alison Weir, amongst others. And the rose, rosa mundi, is named for her. Waterhouse painted her in 1910. His portrait shows her dressed in blue with a white veil kneeling at castle window and looking out at the castle, river, bridge and landscape beyond it. The room's draperies show knights in combat and a tapestry in progress on its frame behind her is of the king and knights in royal progress. Peeking at her around the curtain is (probably) a concerned looking nun. Off to the National Museum in Cardiff if you want to see the rose artfully twined around the window in this beautiful painting. Stay in the museum awhile though and take a look at Rosetti's offering from fifty years earlier. His *Fair Rosamund* is nothing of the sort; it is, yes, a rose strewn portrait, but this lady – all neck, prominent jaw and blubbery lips – is no beauty to my eyes. In fact, it's the worst Rosetti I have ever seen.

HAY'S GREATEST EXPORT

By which I mean, of course, the concept of book town – the regeneration of a town into a tourist destination for (second hand) book lovers with providers of attendant accommodation and purveyors of refreshments. Richard Booth was instrumental in setting up a *village des livres* in Montolieu in the South of France in 1989 and where he spent most of his later years. His daughter ran a café there that transformed into a well-regarded writer's hotel, The International Inkwell, providing accommodation and workshops for writers. Other book towns taking Hay's lead, and which often sought Booth's advice and patronage, including being part of the Commonwealth of book towns with Booth as its International President, rank among their numbers: Redu in Belgium in 1984, Becherel in Brittany, Breedevoort in The Netherlands, St Pierre de Clages in Switzerland and Fountenoy la Joute in France from 1993, and Fjaerland in Norway from 1995, to name but a few.

The concept has even been tried down the road from Hay in the former mining town of Blaenavon, founded in a veritable blaze of publicity in 2003 by American, James Hanna who first opened an erotic bookshop in Hay, and was influenced by Booth. Hanna was jailed as a rapist and child pornographer, and his company folded in 2006 when it was realised that his franchise concept for novice booksellers did not work. His claims to being a business partner of Booth were strongly denied. Happily though, there are five bookshops in Blaenavon still and they are worth calling in on if you are passing or going to the Big Pit mining museum.

There are book towns all over the world from College Street in Kolkata and Paju, South Korea to the gold cities of Grass Valley and Nevada City in Northern California to a host of towns all over Europe. The US's first book town was Stillwater, Minnesota, which links itself to Hay by virtue of its partly Welsh and still Welsh-speaking founding ancestry. Booth tells of an embarrassing

speech made in Welsh at its inauguration. Today the phenomenon is so widespread that, meta though it sounds, books are being written about them. Alex Johnson published one such in 2018,[118] listing some thirty-six book towns worldwide, including Wigtown in Scotland and Sedburgh in the North of England. Hay's boundaries encompass the world; the whole world of the book lover.

Redu is the most special of these book towns as it was twinned with Hay in April 1984. But time passes and interests wane. Despite the weather-worn and decaying wooden surround of the slate plaque depicting a rising trout from the Wye and a wild boar from Belgium, there is not much doing between the two places these days.

TIMBUKTU – FAR, FAR AWAY

More actively, Hay is twinned with Timbuktu. One might at first glance do a double take on that. Why on earth would Hay be twinned with the very definition of somewhere almost mythically far away as a desert town in the middle of Mali? The answer, if you know anything about the well of Buktu's history, past and present, is, of course, books.

Between the thirteenth and sixteenth centuries Timbuktu was a significant seat of Islamic learning with various madrassas making up its university attracting scholars from across the Muslim world. It had a thriving book trade –the salt and gold trading routes also being ink roads – and hundreds of private libraries; the acquisition of books being hugely important to such scholarship. Here we are talking collections of manuscripts setting out Islamic learning in everything from mathematics and astronomy to history and Islamic law, along with copies of the Quran and theological commentaries. These collections are still there, some cached in the baked earth of people's properties, some on shelves in people's homes, in private libraries, and many in the Ahmed Baba Institute[119], which was set up to preserve the texts. It is sometimes hard for its staff to pry them from the hands of their keepers for cataloguing and preservation, but this mammoth task is on going with help from conservators and scholars from across the world, especially from South Africa.

Only a fraction of the texts have been read, let alone studied, let alone translated into English from Arabic or the local languages, interestingly written using Arabic letters. So far the results of this work are rewriting our understanding of the history of Africa and its literary culture. Hundred of thousands of these precious artefacts were saved from the recent occupation of Timbuktu by Daesh forces and thankfully not destroyed when the Institute was set on fire in January 2013. One of its librarians, Asbdel Kader Haidra, spirited away 350,000 mediaeval texts from the Daesh's attentions and only a fraction of these treasures were lost.

The twinning with Hay came in 2007 lead by Anne Brichto of Addyman Books and Hay beat York and Oxford, the other contending towns, for the honour. The mayor of Timbuktu visited Hay that October to sign the declaration of friendship. One of two local charities, Hay2Timbuktu,[120] exists to support educational and health activities in Mali. To date it has funded a girls' school, provided bursaries for girls' education, and various medical and sanitation projects – toilets, a current campaign, are important to keep girls in school and have been built in many of Timbuktu's high schools - working hard to maintain links and provide assistance in the form of both cash and moral support in this still very unstable and dangerous part of the world.

As one wanders around Hay today, the remnants of the, sometimes tenuous, Timbuktu Trail can be spotted at various locations, signalled by a smallish cream sign with a number on it.

If you find yourself at one of these you can ponder the connections, but to save you the effort, here's my take on them.[121]

Start at the Craft Centre on Oxford Road, where the linking theme here is tourism, although this is not of much worth in Timbuktu's case these days given the present security situation, which is highly dangerous.

Stop Two is the Cinema Bookshop on Church Street, obviously for the books. The 1950s building was a cinema for twenty years until it was bought by Richard Booth. At one point it was the largest second hand bookshop in the world, with literally miles of shelving. In 1982 Booth sold it to his long time business rival, Leon Morelli and his Pharos Rare Books. During the 1980s, Morelli bought a number of ailing bookshops in strategic locations, such as the Charing Cross Road and Cambridge, and had three shops in Hay. One of his innovations was to rotate the entire stock between the shops four times a year in order to meet 'what's new' requests; some logistical nightmare with 20,000 books. Morelli organised a mock referendum in Hay in 1984 in which twenty-five per cent of the town voted to end the reign of King Richard and was infamous as the backer of a major retail development that would have brought Tesco to town. Thankfully this met very stiff opposition from townsfolk and shop owners alike and the so-called Plan B to relocate the primary school and redevelop its site did not go ahead. Having pared back his shops as the book trade waned to just two, one each in London and Hay, in July 2016 a consortium of nine employees bought out an unwell Morelli – the businesses, not the buildings. Sadly, very shortly after the sale and his retirement Morelli died.

The Medical Centre on Forest Road is Stop Three. Medics4Timbuktu being instrumentally involved in the projects the town supports there, which have included training midwives and supplying the innovative motorbike ambulance. Apparently there has been little direct involvement recent years due to the significant unrest in Mali, until the pandemic arrived that is and new funds were raised to provide hygiene support there.

Stop Four are the Almshouses on Church Street. These were built in the 1830s for the care of six poor and indigent women and are now Grade two listed. One Frances Harley funded their building in memory of her sister Martha. The women for whom they were intended had to be Hay (or Breconshire) residents over

sixty, widowed or spinsters, members of the Church of England (sic), and of good cleanliness and behaviour. Obviously I'm not going to qualify for such aid anytime soon. By contrast Malian tradition has it that sons care for their elderly mothers at home, a cultural difference worth noting, perhaps.

Swan's Well off Gypsy Castle Lane makes the watery link with Buktu's well, the founding myth of Timbuktu and is Stop Five. It's a quiet place to pause any day and consider the mystery of water emerging from red rock damp enough to accommodate the fleshy lobes of liverwort; essential for life in the desert, but not in short supply in Wales. Stop Five might easily have been Black Lion Well or any of the other seven wells of Hay.

Stop Six is St Mary's Church, the largest of Hay's places of worship a little further down Gypsy Castle Lane. Religion in Timbuktu centres around the Djinguereber Mosque. Built in the early fourteenth century, it was completed in 1327 and is constructed from mud, fibre, straw and wood, and needs repairing annually. It is a world-renowned building, a UNESCO world heritage site, which escaped the Daesh occupation of Timbuktu relatively unscathed, unlike the town's mausoleums, which were systematically wrecked, and one of the city's other mosques which had a fifteenth century door destroyed.

The river Wye along The Warren is Stop Seven. More water. Timbuktu has the river Niger, but that has migrated over the centuries to some twenty kilometres away from the city. The Libyan government paid for a canal to be cut to bring water back to Timbuktu in 2006, but it soon silted up and now only has water for three months of the year.

Stop Eight is Hayfield Community Garden up Bridge Street and over the river, which tested a drip irrigation system for Timbuktu in order to maximise crop yields from minimal water as part of Jump4Timbuktu's[122] sustainability programme. This charity was set up as a fair trade initiative to support Tuareg craftsmen, but also focuses on food security.

St John's Chapel in Lion Street and its history as Pennoyre school in the seventeenth century is Stop Nine. For the education of poor children, its link to Timbuktu is via the Hay2Timbuktu schools programme, focusing on the education of girls who otherwise lose out to their brothers.

Hay Makers on St John's Place sells a range of fairly traded Tuareg silver jewellery and leather goods. Supporting this initiative at Stop Ten and me coming away with something beautiful to wear is a win-win all round, given my penchant for such adornments. This trade not aid initiative is still going strong, despite the current state of affairs in Timbuktu. As Chris Armstrong tells me, it started some ten years ago with the Feldgates, Marie Rogers and Chris working with five craft associations there. A high point in the co-operation was participation at Art in Action in Oxfordshire. This prestigious art and craft fair no longer runs, more's the pity, as it was on my list of must attend venues for many years. In the years that it did raise its tents in the fields next to Waterperry House, the craft goods from Timbuktu were among the stars of the show. Now the trade with Timbuktu is down to just the one determined guild and a trader who has worked to sustain an export business from a war zone, being prepared to travel a thousand miles and wait a week for a visa to visit Britain. Some achievement.

The trail ends at the (former) Council Offices on Broad Street, which housed the offices of Two Towns, One World, the Welsh government and EU funded project to raise awareness and understanding among people in Hay-on-Wye and Powys of global development issues and the UN's Millennium Development Goals for poverty reduction. It's initial grant enabled the two Hay charities to consider and kick start their responses to Timbuktu.

NOTES

1. Christopher Sommerville, *Welsh Borders*, 1991, George Philip, p.70.

2 Kilvert, Rev Francis, *Kilvert's Diary*, Vintage, 2013 entry for 5 April 1870.

3. https://www.thetimes.co.uk/article/oxfam-in-hay-on-wye-changes-locks-and-axes-bloody-welsh-shop-volunteers-nzcgtvfsl

4. Powys was made of the counties Radnorshire, Montgomeryshire and Brecknockshire in the mid 1970s.

5. Quoted by Oliver Balch without reference.

6. Ed. John Davies, Nigel Jenkins, Menna Baines and Peredur I. Lynch, *The Welsh Academy Encylopedia of Wales,* 2008

7. *Kilvert's Diary,* ibid, 22 May 1871

8. Balch, Oliver, *Under the Tump*, 2016, Faber.

9. Noakes, Kate, *Cape Town*, 2011, Eyewear.

10. As Oliver Balch reports, ibid, p.188.

11. Loft, Charles, *Government, the Railways and the Modernisation of Britain,* 2006, Routledge.

12. Betjeman, John, *Collected Poems*, 2006, Hodder & Stoughton.

13. http://www.globeathay.org/

14. An interesting interview with Lawson can be found here https://www.walesartsreview.org/interview-hilary-lawson-director-of-how-the-light-gets-in/

15. https://www.soas.ac.uk/library/archives/collections/missionary-collections/#CouncilforWorldMissionincorporatingtheLondonMissionarySociety

16. http://www.haydialaride.com/

17. http://www.francescakay.co.uk/

18. Thomas, Dylan, *Under Milk Wood,* 1953.

19. Beales, Martin, *The Hay Poisoner,* 2013, PMB press.

20. http://www.coflein.gov.uk/en/site/32549/details/broad-street-clock-tower-hay-on-wye

21. http://savehaylibrary.org/

22. https://christophermeredith.webs.com/

23. https://www.theguardian.com/books/2012/nov/23/protect-our-libraries-jeanette-winterson

24. www.viabeata.co.uk

25. http://www.willspankie.com/

26. 'Lines written a few miles above Tintern Abbey', William Wordsworth, 1798.

27. ibid.

28. *Kilvert's Diary,* ibid, 5 March 1870.

29. Chatwin, Bruce, *On the Black Hill*, 1982, Picador, p.19.

30. Booth, Richard, *My Kingdom of Books,* 1999, Y Lolfa.

31. https://offasdyke.org.uk/offas-dyke-association/offas-dyke-centre/

32 Borrow, George, *Wild Wales*, 1872.

33. www.geocaching.com

34. https://transitionnetwork.org/

35. Noakes, Kate, *The Wall Menders*, 2009, Two Rivers Press.

36. https://churchheritagecymru.org.uk/CHR/ChurchDetails.aspx?id=4373 #Home retrieved October 2018.

37. 'I wandered lonely as a cloud', William Wordsworth.

38. http://folklorethursday.com/regional-folklore/herefordshire-folklore-leg end-black-vaughan-ellen-terrible/#sthash.YHrTk58K.dpbs retrieved 4 November 2017

39. Now Boz Books on Castle Street

40. Booth, *My Kingdom of Books*

41. https://www.h-art.org.uk/explore/venue/jeremy-stiff

42. I recall that famously the M6 toll has a hardcore of pulped Mills and Boons.

43. Quoted by Saikia, page 61.

44. http://daibach-welldigger.blogspot.com/2011/09/methodist-martyr-will iam-seward.html provides a good summary of Seward's life.

45. https://thestoryofbooks.com/blog/

46. https://www.haycheesemarket.org/cic

47. Kilvert's Diary, 14 October 1870.

48. Rosetti, Christina, *Poems and Prose*, Everyman, 1994

49. Haslam, Richard, *The Buildings of Wales – Powys*, Penguin, 1979 quoted by Saunders.

50. http://www.roll-of-honour.com/Breconshire/Hay.html

51. Gill, Eric, *Autobiography*, 1940, Cape quoted in Miles, Jonathan, *Try the Wilderness First*, 2018, Seren.

52. Basic historical details can be found here https://britishlistedbuildings .co.uk/300007380-st-johns-chapel-hay#.XFicvS10eu4

53. www.chaptershayonwye.co.uk

54. Gaudy facts are in the main from Jennifer Lewis with thanks http:// www.interpretingceramics.com/issue013/articles/02.htm

55. Murray, Nicholas, *Crossings: A Journey through Borders,* 2016, Seren.

56. Murray, ibid. p.158

57. A note on the Ordinance Survey maps that include Hay – for a proper view you need two sheets of the 1:50,000 series, numbers 161 and 148, as Hay and its environs are appropriately, but annoyingly, only fully covered by both. The fate of a border town, perhaps, but more likely just where the

OS decided to draw its lines.

58. The Marcher Lords were warlords appointed by the Norman kings of England to carve out territory and profitable fiefdoms for themselves in Wales. This system of government was advantageous to the English crown as the lords' land grab cost the monarchy nothing (they raised their own armies), potential rivals could be kept at arm's length, and inter-marriage with the Welsh nobility strengthened Angevin influence.

59. According to Gerald of Wales' chronicle. Gerald came to Wales in 1188 with the Archbishop of Canterbury to recruit for the Third Crusade.

60. http://www.barbara-erskine.co.uk/novels/novels/lady-of-hay/lady-of-hay -research-notes.htm

61. Camden wrote *Britain, or a Chronological Description of the most Flourishing Kingdomes, England, Scotland, and Ireland*; Wales having been absorbed into England by this time, at least in Camden's imaginings.

62. Murray, ibid, p.158..

63. http://www.april-ashley.com/

64. http://www.liverpoolmuseums.org.uk/mol/exhibitions/april-ashley/index .aspx

65. www.haycastletrust.org

66. Rumour has it that Prince Charles admired the castle's roll top bath, which subsequently found its way to Dumfries House. It is not known if any sums changed hands.

67. Gerald of Wales, *The Journey Through Wales*, 1988, Penguin.

68. As noted in 1809 by Tobias Jones in his *History of Brecknockshire*, p.596.

69. Much of this relies on Hub, Tobias, B, *Imposters in Early Modern England: Representations and Perceptions of Fraudulent Identities*, Manchester University Press, 2009

70. Reported by James Boswell in the notes to his Life of Dr. Johnson of 1791.

71. https://founders.archives.gov/documents/Washington/05-03-02-0101

72. Sheers, Owen, *The Blue Book*, Seren, 2002.

73. Sheers, Owen, *Skirrid Hill*, Seren, 2005.

74. The painting is in the collection of the National Library of Wales.

75. MacCarthy, Fiona, *Eric Gill*, 1990, Faber

76. Lord, Peter, *The Tradition – A New History of Welsh Art 1400-1990*, 2016, Parthian p.272 et seq.

77. A good chronology of Gill and Jones' time at Capel y Ffin is Miles, Jonathan, *Try the Wilderness First: Eric Gill & David Jones at Capel-y-Ffin*, Seren, 2018.

78. Quoted by Miles, ibid, page 55

79. Jones, David, *In Parenthesis*, 1937, Faber, p.77.

80. Jones, David, *In Parenthesis*, 1937, Faber.

81. Not to be confused with the Priory of the same name further down the valley.

82. Kilvert, ibid, 2 September 1870.

83. Kilvert, ibid, 5 April 1870.

84. Precised from Lyne's Wikipedia page retrieved December 2017.

85. http://www.fatherignatius.org.uk/the-pilgrimage/ retrieved December 2017.

86. http://www.fatherignatius.org.uk/the-pilgrimage/ retrieved 1 January 2018.

87. Meredith, Christopher, *Air Histories*, 2013, Seren.

88. Ravilious, Eric, *Travelling Artist: 4*, The Mainstone Press.

89. Ginsberg, Allen, *Wales Visitation*, Five Seasons Press, 1979

90. http://www.academia.edu/25804747/Allen_Ginsberg_s_Wales_Visitati on_as_a_neo-Romantic_response_to_Wordsworth_s_Tintern_Abbey_

91. https://www.youtube.com/watch?v=eKBAJYceQ54

92. First published in *I-spy and shanty*, corrupt press, 2014.

93. https://www.tate.org.uk/art/artworks/turner-llanthony-abbey-d00679

94. https://en.wikipedia.org/wiki/Llanthony_Priory

95. Colvin, Sidney, *Landor*, CUP, 1881.

96. https://www.theguardian.com/books/2017/mar/03/books-readers-neve r-had-so-good-hay-festival-director-trust-storytellers-politicians

97. https://www.indexoncensorship.org/2017/01/volume-45-04-magazine-hay-festival-director-on-global-challenges-of-freedom-of-speech/

98. https://www.theguardian.com/books/2021/aug/01/hay-festival-in-disar ray-as-director-quits-after-bullying-claim-upheld

99. https://www.youtube.com/user/HayLevels

100. https://nation.cymru/culture/poor-taffs-festival-or-is-hay-really-in-wal es/

101. https://www.indexoncensorship.org/2017/01/volume-45-04-magazine-hay-festival-director-on-global-challenges-of-freedom-of-speech/

102. https://www.nytimes.com/2020/10/19/world/middleeast/hay-festival-abu-dhabi-sexual-assault.html

103. https://www.hayfestival.com/hayplayer/?skinid=16&localesetting=en-G B

104. First published in Noakes, Kate, *Ocean to Interior,* Mighty Erudite, 2007.

105 Also available in my first proper collection, *Ocean to Interior,* Mighty Erudite, 2007 and sadly now out of print, but possibly to be found on a shelf somewhere in Hay, if one was to search for long enough.

106. Today the Glanusk estate is owned by the Legg-Bourkes — daughter Tiggy having been nanny to Princes William and Harry; mother Shân is Lord

Lieutenant of Powys and Lady in Waiting to the Princess Royal.

107. https://stmaryschurchhayonwye.co.uk/

108. A Record of the Gravestones, Tombs & Monuments in Saint Mary's Churchyard Hay-on-Wye.

109. Strictly, novelist Rafael Sabatini was his step-father.

110. Mother made this in sorrow.

111. Saunders, ibid, page 69.

112. *Kilvert's Diary*, ibid, 3 March 1878.

113. See Weir, Anthony and Jerman, James, *Images of Lust: Sexual Carvings on Medieval Churches*, Batsford, 1986, amongst others.

114. McMahon, Joanne and Roberts, Jack, *The Sheela-na-gigs of Ireland and Britain: the Divine Hags of the Christian Celts – an Illustrated Guide*, 2000, Mercier.

115. http://cusophistory.wixsite.com/cusop

116. http://www.nicolahopwood.co.uk/

117. http://www.whitneybridge.co.uk/about#history

118. Johnson, Alex, Book Towns, Francis Lincoln, 2018.

119. https://www.tombouctoumanuscripts.org/libraries/ahmed_baba_institute_of_higher_learning_and_islamic_research_iheri-ab/

120. http://hay2timbuktu.org/

121. With some help from Eigon at http://lifeinhay.blogspot.com/2013/05/timbuktu-trail.html

122. https://www.jump4timbuktu.org/index.php

WORKS CONSULTED

I am indebted to all who have written about Hay and its environs before me in fact and fiction, in particular:

Balch, Oliver, *Under the Tump, Sketches of Real Life on the Welsh Borders*, 2016, Faber.

Booth, Richard, *My Kingdom of Books*, 1999, Y Lolfa.

Chatwin, Bruce, *On the Black Hill*, 1982, Picador.

Kilvert, Francis, *Kilvert's Diary 1870-1879*, 2013, Vintage.

Miles, Jonathan, *Try the Wilderness First: Eric Gill & David Jones at Capel-y-ffin*, 2018, Seren.

Murray, Nicholas, *Crossings: A Journey through Borders*, 2016, Seren.

Saunders, Jim, *Hay: Landscape, Literature and the Town of Books*, 2014, Seren.

Saikia, Robin, *Hay on Wye*, 2010, Blue Guide.

THE PHOTOGRAPHS

ACKNOWLEDGEMENTS

Thanks in huge measure to everyone who talked to me about Hay and other matters that have informed this book including: Jasper Fforde, Sarah Rowland-Jones, Chris and Melanie Prince, Peter Florence, Chris Armstrong, Ros and Geoff Garratt, and Trudy Stedman. Many thanks to series editor, Peter Finch, for trusting me to write to the edge of and over the page. And finally, I am grateful to my parents for taking me to Hay and indulging my bookish passions. This book is for them.

THE AUTHOR

Kate Noakes is primarily known as a poet. She has degrees in Geography, and English Literature from the University of Reading, and an MPhil in Creative Writing from the University of South Wales. She is researching a PhD at Reading in contemporary British and American poetry. She was elected to The Welsh Academy in 2011 and her website (www.boomslangpoetry.blogspot.com) is archived by the National Library of Wales. Her poetry collections include *Ocean to Interior, The Wall Menders, Cape Town, I-spy and shanty, Tattoo on Crow Street, Paris Stage Left,* and *The Filthy Quiet.*

Kate can trace her Welsh heritage to the sixteenth century in the Vale of Glamorgan and has ancestors from Carmarthenshire, Cardiganshire and Breconshire. The many times great-granddaughter of Welsh language poet and hymn writer, Siôn Llewelyn (1690-1776), she lives in London where she reviews poetry for *Poetry Wales, Poetry London, The North* and *London Grip,* and acts as a trustee to London writer development organisation, Spread the Word. She is a frequent visitor to Hay.

INDEX